SALT *to* TASTE

100+ Protein and Salt-Rich Recipes for a Happier, Healthier You

DR. JAMES DINICOLANTONIO
& TRICIA WILLIAMS

VICTORY BELT PUBLISHING INC.
LAS VEGAS

First published in 2025 by Victory Belt Publishing Inc.

ISBN-13: 978-1-628605-36-5

Cover and interior design by Kat Lannom

Cover photo by Megan DiNicolantonio

Illustrations by Crizalie Olimpo and Elita San Juan

Food photography by Tatiana Briceag

Printed in Canada

TC 0125

TABLE *of* CONTENTS

INTRODUCTION

Salt Your Way to Health

Salting food to taste is something many of us do without giving it much thought. Not only does salt enhance the flavor of food by cutting the bitterness and enhancing the sweetness, but it also provides essential minerals that our bodies need to function. It is so important that our bodies are designed to crave it!

Salt goes hand in hand with protein, which is the primary key to satiety. Most of the protein in your diet should come from animal foods, which have more bioavailable protein and other nutrients than plant foods. The recipes in this book are all about combining nutritious proteins with the ideal amount of salt. They also supply healthy fats and a moderate amount of healthy carbohydrates to deliver a balanced diet that allows for sustainable fat loss so you'll feel better than ever.

The idea is to consume meals that keep you satisfied and well nourished so you're not constantly hungry throughout the day. This cookbook includes 100-plus recipes to do just that. We want it to be your guide to eating healthier meals, and we hope you will use it for years to come.

A NOTE FROM *Dr. DiNicolantonio*

My grandmother always used to say, "Health is wealth." One of the things that sticks out to me about her is how she focused on eating quality food. Healthy eating was very important to her, and that's why she cooked almost all her meals at home. One of my fondest memories of her is how she would pack a slice of white bread into a ball in her hand and say to me, "You see this? This is not real bread." You could say that I get my love of food and cooking from her.

Food is more than just enjoyment; it is medicine. What you put on your fork largely determines which diseases you will or won't get. We need to shift focus away from immediate pleasure to the long-term health consequences of our food choices. If you mostly eat the way our ancestors ate—consuming only foods you could hunt or pick from the earth—then you have a much better chance of living a long and healthy life than someone who eats primarily processed foods.

The recipes in this cookbook are meant to nourish your brain and body. The recipes focus on nutrient-dense, flavorful meals rather than low-calorie bland food. We hope that whenever you need a healthy, tasty meal, you will pull a recipe from this book and start cooking.

A NOTE FROM *Tricia Williams*

What you put on your fork has the power to change everything! My culinary journey began in the bustling kitchens of fine dining establishments in New York City, where I honed my skills and developed a deep passion for creating beautiful dishes. However, it wasn't until 2005, when I became pregnant, that my relationship with food took on a new meaning.

Reading Michael Pollan's book *The Omnivore's Dilemma* was a turning point in my life. It opened my eyes to the profound connection between our food, how it's grown and raised, and its effect on our health and the environment. This led me to rethink not only what I put on my plate but also the values and principles guiding my choices. I began to nourish myself and my son with food sourced from organic, regenerative farms. I choose local, whole, and natural ingredients that honor both our bodies and the planet.

These principles have since become the foundation of how I live my life and run my business. I believe that healthful eating should be a beautiful, delicious, and celebratory experience at every meal. Eating is about more than nutrition; it's about gathering around the dinner table, sharing food prepared with love, and engaging in meaningful conversations that connect us with each other and the world around us.

In this book, I've poured my heart and soul into recipes that I hope will inspire you to do just that. Whether you're preparing a meal for yourself or a feast for loved ones, I want you to feel the joy and satisfaction that comes from eating well. I hope this book will serve as a guide and a source of inspiration as you embark on your journey of nourishing yourself and those you care about with beautiful, delicious food.

ALL ABOUT *Salt*

Salty is one of the five tastes, along with sweet, sour, bitter, and umami, and salt is the only essential mineral with a taste receptor on the tongue. There's a good reason for this. Salt is the most consequential mineral we lose through sweat, and we can quickly become depleted of it. Sodium deficiency can be deadly. That's why the human body, like the bodies of other mammals, has a way to ensure that if you need salt, you eat more of it. If you become deficient, the dopamine reward center in your brain gets hyperactivated, making you crave salt. Once you consume salt, you get a greater reward from it, preventing you from dying of salt deficiency.

What is salt, and how much do you need?

Salt is made up of two essential minerals: sodium and chloride. Sodium helps hydrate your body, allows neurons to fire, and helps muscles contract. Chloride aids digestion by contributing to the production of hydrochloric acid and enables immune cells to fight off pathogens by helping to produce hypochlorous acid.

Ideal salt intake can vary greatly from person to person. However, for normal healthy adults, most clinical studies and observational studies suggest that 1⅓ to 2⅓ teaspoons of salt (containing 3,000 to 5,300 milligrams of sodium) per day is optimal.

Many public health organizations recommend that people consume less salt than this, but we believe their advice is misguided. Why? Because most other biomarkers (like insulin, cholesterol, and triglycerides) and stress hormones (like aldosterone, noradrenaline, and adrenaline) increase on a low-salt diet. Plus, the suggestion that our ancestors had a low salt intake does not consider the salt they would have obtained by eating nose to tail, which would have included the salty blood and interstitial fluid (a fluid that surrounds cells) of the animals they hunted and consumed. They also would have followed animals to salt licks or brackish (somewhat salty) water sources. Many publications suggest that around 65 percent of caloric intake came from plant foods. However, substantial data suggests that *at least* 65 percent came from animal foods, and some data indicates the amount was close to 100 percent in circumpolar populations.[1] Thus, the hypothesis that Paleolithic humans consumed only 700 milligrams of sodium per day is likely an underestimate. Furthermore, even if our predecessors did consume little salt, that doesn't mean their intake was optimal for human health. They did whatever they could to survive.

Another consideration regarding salt requirements is that most people lose around 1,200 milligrams of sodium per hour of exercise and another 1,200 milligrams of sodium per 4 cups of coffee (the equivalent of 360 milligrams of caffeine).[2] Certain medications, especially diuretics, increase the need for salt. So, if you are active, drink a lot of coffee, or take medications such as a diuretic, you may need even more salt.

What are the benefits of a normal salt intake?

When people switch from a processed to a whole-food diet, salt intake often decreases. Because meat no longer comes with the salty blood, even animal-based whole-food diets lack salt. Consequently, you must add salt when you eat a whole-food diet.

Salt is necessary to provide sodium for action potentials so your heart can beat and for neurotransmitter function to enable you to move your muscles. An adequate sodium intake also provides the following benefits:

- **Helps keep your body hydrated:** Salt increases thirst, which encourages you to drink more fluids. Most older adults lose their thirst signal and underconsume water, which leads to dehydration. Adding salt to the diet helps stimulate thirst, which improves water intake and decreases the risk of dehydration. Salt also improves the absorption and retention of water and helps move water where it needs to go in the body. Sodium is osmotic, meaning water follows sodium. Having enough sodium in your blood allows for adequate blood volume to perfuse all your organs so they function properly.

- **Allows you to exercise:** One of the first signs of not having enough salt is exercise intolerance.

- **Reduces muscle cramps:** When you exercise, you lose a lot of salt through sweat, which can lead to muscle cramps. The average person loses 1,200 milligrams of sodium (half a teaspoon of salt) per hour of exercise.

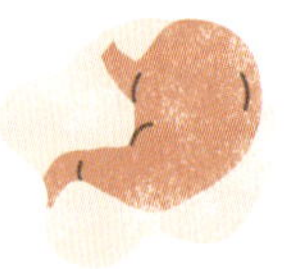

- **Improves digestion:** The chloride in salt helps make hydrochloric acid in the stomach, facilitating digestion and the assimilation of nutrients.

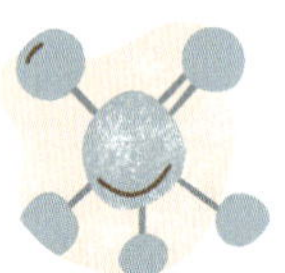

- **Keeps minerals in balance:** When you don't get enough salt, your body pulls sodium, magnesium, and calcium from bone. In other words, insufficient salt can lead to negative calcium and magnesium balance and worsening bone health.

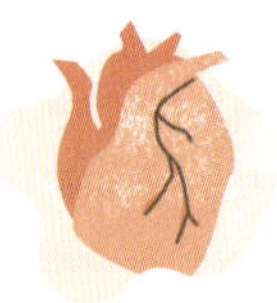

- **Decreases heart rate, stress hormones, insulin, cholesterol, and triglycerides:** Low salt is viewed as a stressful situation, and your body upregulates many hormones to try to retain salt from your diet. Medications are used to block these stress hormones (like angiotensin-II, renin, and aldosterone) to lower cardiovascular events, but ensuring a normal salt intake is the more natural way to do it.

What is the harm of not getting enough salt?

Not getting enough salt has a wide range of negative consequences, including the following:

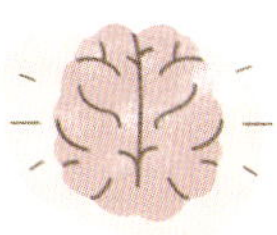

- **Causes cravings:** As mentioned earlier, the dopamine reward center in your brain becomes hyperactivated when you don't get enough sodium, increasing both salt cravings and the dopamine release that occurs when you finally consume salt. Unfortunately, not getting enough salt also increases the dopamine release in the brain when you consume sugars and processed carbohydrates, leading to cravings for those foods.

- **Leads to overeating of processed foods:** The cravings for salt, sugar, and processed carbohydrates can lead to overeating processed foods that contain these things, which explains why people who don't eat enough salt can end up overeating things like pretzels or potato chips.

- **Leads to dehydration:** Dehydration causes the arteries to constrict and can increase blood pressure. Additionally, dehydration may increase hunger and urge you to eat so your body can get water from the food, contributing to the overeating issue mentioned in the preceding bullet.

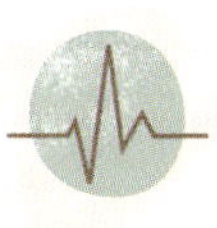

- **Increases heart rate:** Not getting enough salt drops blood volume, which leads to an increase in heart rate to compensate for the lower blood pressure. This is a stressful situation for the heart.

- **Leads to insulin resistance:** At least twenty-three human clinical studies show that low-salt diets increase insulin levels and insulin resistance.[3] Thus, not getting enough salt from the diet may increase the amount of fat stored per calorie consumed. Insulin resistance can also lead to leptin resistance and constant hunger, which occurs with the overconsumption of refined sugars. However, insufficient salt can lead to a similar pathway that stimulates increased hunger. Salting your food to taste helps ensure that insulin and leptin levels remain sensitive, and your hunger signals remain optimized.

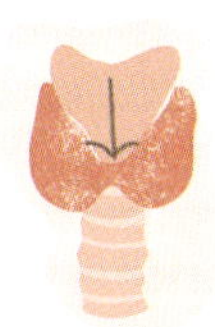

- **Increases the risk of iodine deficiency and hypothyroidism:** Insufficient salt intake can lead to iodine deficiency. Iodine is an essential mineral for making thyroid hormones, which determine your basal metabolic rate. Not getting enough salt can lead to hypothyroidism, a decrease in your metabolic rate, and an increase in the propensity for weight gain. This issue is further enhanced when you sweat because people lose around 50 to 100 micrograms of iodine per liter of sweat. You need to ingest around 150 micrograms of iodine daily, and certain natural salts contain natural iodine. Eating a normal amount of salt that contains some iodine can help ensure your body gets enough of this essential mineral so the main metabolism hormones (thyroid hormones) work properly. Thus, the two main hormones that control fat gain—insulin and thyroid hormones—are adversely affected by low-salt diets. Many people suffer from low thyroid or insulin resistance and don't even realize it. They try cutting calories or working out more but don't seem to lose weight. Simply ensuring a good intake of sodium and iodine may help improve those fat-regulating hormones and make weight loss easier.

- **Reduces energy and activity levels:** Low-salt diets can lead to dehydration, insulin resistance, and low thyroid function, which stimulate the body to move less. Additionally, low-salt diets cause exercise intolerance. Adding appropriate amounts of salt to your diet will help improve hydration and energy levels and dramatically increase your athletic performance. All of this helps improve weight loss. If you don't have enough salt in your body, your body isn't going to want to move and sweat as much because it doesn't have the salt necessary to continue copious amounts of activity and sweating. Thus, if you want to improve the signaling to your body to move and sweat more, you need to have good amounts of salt in the diet.

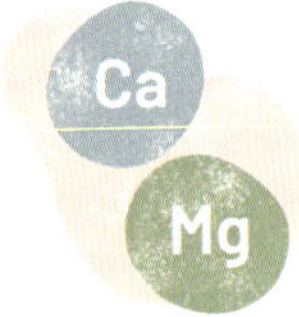

- **Leads to mineral imbalances:** When your body doesn't get enough salt, it excretes about four times more calcium and magnesium in sweat to preserve sodium.[4] There is also a reduction in gastrointestinal absorption of magnesium and calcium on low-salt diets. When you don't get enough salt, your body pulls sodium from bone to try to maintain adequate sodium levels. Magnesium and calcium get pulled along with sodium, spiking calcium and magnesium levels in your blood. The elevated blood levels of calcium and magnesium cause a compensatory reduction in the absorption of these minerals from the intestine and increased elimination in the urine, leading to a negative magnesium and calcium balance.

Low-salt diets (less than 2,300 milligrams of sodium per day) have been shown to worsen sleep, energy levels, and exercise tolerance. Other side effects include headaches, inability to focus, erectile dysfunction, insulin resistance, high insulin levels, elevated triglycerides, and elevated artery-stiffening hormones like aldosterone, angiotensin-II, and renin, which can even cause acute kidney failure. The reason low-salt diets can cause kidney failure is because they can drop blood volume so much that perfusion of organs, including the kidney, can go down, causing acute kidney failure. Essentially, low-salt diets are simply causing people to become dehydrated because their blood volume drops, which then causes all the vasoconstrictive/artery-stiffening hormones to increase to compensate for the low blood volume.

Low-salt diets also reduce the activity of brown adipose tissue, which is the good fat that helps you "burn calories" by releasing heat energy.[5] Indeed, in the same study, low-salt diets caused animals to gain fat. Thus, low-salt diets may lower your basal metabolic rate and the activity of your brown fat and raise fatty acid synthesis, contributing to accelerated fat gain.

How should you get salt?

The best way to get salt is to use unrefined sea salt on your food. In other words, salt to taste. Dr. DiNicolantonio likes Redmond Real Salt because its source is an ancient dried-up ocean, and it's extracted from 700 feet below ground. Thus, it's sheltered from the microplastics and modern-day contamination that affect salts sourced from other oceans.

Refined salts are bleached white and use very high-heat processing, whereas Redmond salt, which is unrefined, does not go through these processes. Additionally, Redmond salt contains natural iodine. Based on its mineral analysis, 10 grams of Redmond salt contains about 170 micrograms of iodine. However, the company does not artificially add potassium iodide, so the FDA makes the company state "not a good source of iodide" on the label.

Most of the recipes in this book call for adding salt to enhance the flavor, but feel free to dial up or down the amount of salt based on your taste preferences.

ALL ABOUT *Protein*

Protein is the building block of life. It's the second largest component of human tissue after water. Muscles, skin, hair, nails, organs, and bones are all made from protein. Protein is composed of amino acids, the structural units of all cells. Amino acids are necessary for cellular energy metabolism, neurotransmitter transport and biosynthesis, and tissue repair and growth. The richest protein sources are meat, eggs, and fish, but it is also found in nuts, seeds, legumes, and vegetables. One gram of protein is said to provide four calories, but about 25 to 30 percent of the calories are used simply to digest protein in the body.

You need adequate protein intake to maintain a certain amount of body weight and lean tissue. If you eat less protein than your body needs or fast for a long time, you will gradually lose weight because of the lack of amino acid building blocks and lower levels of protein synthesis. During exercise and high physical activity, your body's demand for protein is even higher than at rest. Calorie restriction also increases body protein loss by raising protein oxidation.

The daily sum of protein degradation and synthesis is called *protein turnover.* In the average person, 300 to 400 grams of protein are degraded and synthesized daily. The rate of protein turnover is insensitive to protein intake. In other words, the amount of turnover is determined by your overall body weight, amount of muscle, and activity level, not by how much protein you eat. Protein breakdown increases while you're fasting and exercising, and synthesis occurs when you eat protein. Resistance training increases protein breakdown, but protein synthesis rises even more, leading to a net positive balance if protein intake is appropriate.

The following things promote protein synthesis:

- Eating protein
- Consuming protein powder
- Consuming essential amino acid supplements
- Meeting the leucine threshold
- Resistance training
- Ingesting carbohydrates post-exercise

These things reduce protein breakdown:

- Eating protein
- Consuming protein powder
- Consuming essential amino acids

And these things increase protein breakdown:

- Calorie restriction
- Extended fasting
- Cardio exercise
- Resistance training
- Stress hormones (cortisol and adrenaline)
- Sedentarism

Your body has limited sites for long-term storage of protein. Shortly after protein is digested, amino acids circulate throughout the body in the blood and lymphatic system. This supply—a few hundred calories' worth of amino acids—is called the *amino acid pool,* and it lasts until those amino acids have been used. Temporary protein stores fluctuate throughout the day, and they're connected to feeding-fasting cycles. That is why it's more important for overall health and performance to obtain dietary protein more frequently than carbohydrates or fats.

What is a high-protein diet?

A high protein intake means consuming between 1 and 1.25 grams of protein per pound of lean body weight (lean body weight = total body weight - body fat) daily. For most people, that means eating around 30 to 60 grams of protein three to four times a day. Getting 20 to 25 percent of your calories from protein is considered safe and is a good range to aim for.[6] Athletes, especially strength and power athletes, and older people require even more protein.

Most, if not all, of the protein you consume should be from animal foods because the nutrients in animal protein are more bioavailable than those in plant protein, which means that animal protein is more readily used by the body than plant protein. For example, the preformed version of vitamin A (retinol) comes from animal foods, while beta-carotene comes from plant foods. Many people can't turn beta-carotene into vitamin A, so eating animal foods offers an advantage over plant foods. Vitamin K2, creatine, taurine, carnitine, B12, and B2 come from consuming animal foods, but those nutrients are low or nonexistent in plant foods. Also, there is a higher amount of leucine in animal protein than plant protein on a gram-for-gram basis, and leucine is the main amino acid that stimulates muscle protein synthesis.

Animal foods can provide you with all the nutrients you need if you eat nose to tail, but to hit optimal intakes of certain nutrients, like calcium, you also need to consume dairy or eggshells/small bones/bone meal. Another example is vitamin C: hitting your optimal values requires eating certain organs or consuming fruits or 100 percent freshly squeezed orange juice.

Be cautious about consuming too much protein. When protein intake exceeds 40 percent of daily calories, diarrhea, weight loss, and failure to thrive can occur.

How a high-animal-protein diet brings an acid load

Animal protein is high in the sulfur-containing amino acids methionine and cysteine. When you consume animal protein, those amino acids are oxidized in the liver, and sulfuric acid forms; the sulfuric acid then dissociates to a negatively charged sulfate and two hydrogen ions (the latter of which makes your body more acidic). To neutralize the extra acid, your body's bicarbonate stores become depleted, and you lose more positively charged minerals to eliminate the sulfate until your kidneys can make more ammonia/ammonium to help get rid of the negatively charged sulfate. Ammonia is a toxic substance to the kidneys, and 80 percent of the ammonium that hits the collecting duct in the kidneys is from the secretion of ammonia and hydrogen ions at the loop of Henle in the kidneys.

Thus, if you don't offset animal protein with a base, you must produce a lot more ammonia. You also must break down glutamine and glycine to form ammonium/ammonia. You should offset animal protein with fruits and vegetables or bicarbonate/citrate supplements; otherwise, your body has to break down skeletal muscle and connective tissue to get the glutamine/glycine to produce ammonium. Additionally, people on a high-acid-producing diet have less citrate in their urine, which can increase the risk of oxalate kidney stones. The increased acid excretion through the urine also increases uric acid levels and the propensity for uric acid kidney stones.

Consuming a high dietary acid load also increases the production of cortisol, which signals skeletal muscle and connective tissue breakdown. Elevated cortisol can increase insulin resistance.

The costs of producing and excreting high amounts of acid from the kidneys when eating a high-animal-protein diet that's not offset by some type of base include the following:

- Increased production of ammonia
- Greater loss of positively charged minerals like sodium, potassium, magnesium, and calcium
- Increased bone breakdown due to an increase in interstitial fluid acidity, which activates osteoclasts to break down bone and decreases the activation of osteoblasts to build bone
- Greater loss of calcium due to the hyperfiltration at the kidney level due to the high acid load
- Increased insulin resistance due to interstitial fluid acidity
- Increased joint pain due to more acidic interstitial and synovial fluids
- Increased propensity for calcium oxalate and uric acid kidney stones[7,8]

In the 1960s, the Lennon and Lemann group discovered that when subjects excreted around 40 mEq of acid via the kidneys, over half the population retained some acid, which then had to be buffered in some way.[9,10] Many studies have shown negative calcium balance, worsening calcium balance, increased propensity for kidney stones, increased markers of bone breakdown, and decreased markers of bone formation on a high-animal-protein or carnivore diet.[11-18] The Lemann and Lennon group also showed that bone breakdown and calcium loss is part of this buffering system against high dietary acid loads.[19]

A typical standard American diet leads to a net acid excretion of 50 to 100 mEq of acid, and a carnivore diet can lead to a net acid excretion of up to 250 mEq per day. That means that these diets can lead to acid retention. The studies showed that the bone, skeletal muscle, and connective tissues are used to buffer some of this acid, but what those tissues can do isn't enough to prevent a slow accumulation of hydrogen ions in the blood and interstitial fluid. That's why studies of high-animal-protein diets show an increase in steady-state hydrogen ion concentration even after only a few weeks on a high-animal-protein diet.[20] Unfortunately, the interstitial fluid becomes more acidic than the blood because the interstitial fluid does not have the buffering systems the blood has to bind hydrogen ions.[21] The hemoglobin and albumin in the blood can help bind and mask the elevations in hydrogen ions, whereas the interstitial fluid doesn't have this ability. The rise in interstitial acidity affects all cellular receptor functions that face the interstitial fluid, like insulin and thyroid hormone receptors. However, cell receptors can only function within a very narrow pH range; even small changes can affect receptor function. The elevation in interstitial fluid acidity can cause joint and back pain, and taking supplements that improve the alkalinity in the body has been shown to reduce pain.[22]

Some of these effects may take a long time to become apparent, but many people on very low-carb diets, such as carnivore and keto, find that their fasting blood sugar increases, they have less energy to exercise, and their joints hurt. Metabolic ward studies and other clinical studies in humans have proven that carnivore diets cause negative calcium balance, an increase in bone breakdown, and a decrease in bone formation makers. (See the video entitled "High Animal Protein Increases the Propensity for Negative Calcium Balance. Balance It with Base!" on Dr. DiNicolantonio's YouTube channel for coverage of about a dozen human clinical studies on this subject.)

How to offset the acid load from animal foods

Consuming low-oxalate fruits and vegetables helps optimize the benefits of a high-animal-protein diet. High-oxalate foods do not provide much alkalinity to the body because the oxalate prevents the breakdown of the potassium salts (potassium citrate), preventing the liberation of bicarbonate in the body, and bicarbonate is what helps offset the acid load of animal foods. High-oxalate fruits include pomegranates, raspberries, and blackberries, and examples of high-oxalate vegetables are spinach, Swiss chard, rhubarb, soybeans, and the skins of potatoes. Also, limit Brazil nuts and almonds. You don't necessarily have to avoid these foods completely, but you shouldn't count them as offsetting the acid load of animal foods.

You need to consume two to three times more fruits and vegetables than animal foods on a gram-for-gram basis to offset the acid load from animal foods. If you can't consume this quantity of fruits and vegetables to fully offset the acid load from animal foods, supplements like sodium/potassium bicarbonate can help. Dr. DiNicolantonio prefers to take a professional-grade bicarbonate supplement rather than baking soda, which can contain aluminum and is harshly processed. The bicarb formula that he uses can be found via the Fullscript link in his Instagram bio @drjamesdinic. He takes three or four capsules with each of his animal-based meals to offset the acid load.

What are the benefits of eating a high-animal-protein diet?

A diet rich in animal protein provides highly bioavailable protein and nutrients to help with hunger regulation, muscle growth and maintenance, and overall health. When you eat enough bioavailable protein, as found in animal foods, weight loss becomes effortless because you're no longer hungry all the time.

Protein is vital not only for health but also for physical performance. It's an essential nutrient that carries out numerous processes inside the body, and it's directly responsible for many of the adaptations induced by exercise, especially resistance training. Studies consistently show that increased protein intake results in greater muscle growth, strength, and body composition.

Higher protein intake during dieting promotes weight loss, helps maintain muscle mass, and keeps your metabolic rate up. When people are allowed to eat as much as they want on a diet consisting of 30 percent protein, they consume an average of 441 fewer calories a day than when they eat only 10 percent protein.[23] Individuals who eat a high-protein meal burn more calories for several hours after eating.[24] The higher thermic effect of protein also contributes to greater feelings of satiety and fullness.[25] If you take two calorically restricted diets with the same amount of calories but one has higher protein, the higher protein diet will lead to more caloric restriction because of this burn-off effect.

Eating 30 to 60 grams of protein daily also helps ensure hormone health. When you don't get enough protein, hormones like thyroid hormone and insulin may not function appropriately. Eating enough protein can provide some insulin signaling to help with electrolyte retention, but only if the acid load is offset by some form of base from fruits, vegetables, bicarbonate mineral waters, or bicarbonate/citrate supplements. The reason is the acid load can cause an increase in sodium loss from the body due to the hyperfiltration at the kidney level.

It's important to balance a high-animal-protein diet with some type of base. Eating nose to tail provides the base in the form of bicarbonate in blood and interstitial fluid, in bone and bone marrow, in natural mineral waters that contain bicarbonate, and in bicarbonate-forming substances in fruit and tubers. Because we no longer consume blood or interstitial fluid, eating some fruit and vegetables can help offset the acid load of animal foods.

The benefits of protein for weight loss

The number of calories directed toward breaking down protein is anywhere from 20 to 30 percent of total calories in protein. Thus, protein has a lower calorie load than most people realize because the body uses a lot of calories to digest protein, particularly animal protein.

Additionally, protein is the nutrient that contributes most to long-term satiety. If you don't get enough protein, usually around 30 to 60 grams per meal, you will continue to have food cravings to get the protein your body demands.

Is red meat bad for you?

Studies that include processed meats, like bacon that contains nitrates/nitrites, sausage, and lunch meat, associate a higher intake of red meat with poor health outcomes. These associative studies link red meat with cancer or other issues, but they can't prove causation and certainly do not apply to someone eating mostly 100 percent grass-fed meat and dairy or pasture-raised eggs. The quality of the protein matters.

Also, most meat intake in the United States comes with grains, like the bread for a sub sandwich or a burger bun and fries. Sometimes it comes with sugar, like soda. It's hard to tease out all these confounding factors to know if even the poor-quality meat is as bad as it's made out to be. Regardless, most animal protein intake should come from 100 percent grass-fed meat because grain-fed meat and fat can contain harmful chemicals that are sprayed on the grains the cows eat. Additionally, consuming grain makes the cows sick, and the meat contains significantly more fat and fewer antioxidants because grass provides cows and the meat or dairy fat that comes from them with more beta-carotene, vitamin E, and other antioxidants. The omega-3 to omega-6 ratio is also higher in grass-fed or wild meat than in grain-fed meat.

Why should you add salt to protein?

One reason you should add salt to animal protein is because eating animal protein increases your need for salt. The high acid load that animal protein brings into the body is excreted in the urine, which leads to sodium loss via the urine.[26] Blood flow to the kidneys is increased to handle the high acid load, causing hyperfiltration and natriuresis (urinary sodium loss). There is also decreased sodium reabsorption at the kidney level. Thus, neglecting to salt your animal foods can decrease your sodium status. That's why the recipes in this book combine salt with animal protein—to help maintain a good salt status in the body.

WHAT ABOUT *Carbs?*

How many carbohydrates should you eat?

Carbohydrate intake should be tailored to you and your activity level. Some people do better on a very-low-carbohydrate (less than 60 grams of carbs/day) or carnivore-type diet, whereas others who are more active tend to do better eating 100 to 200 grams of carbohydrates per day (or even as high as 300 to 400 grams per day for elite athletes). Thus, your carbohydrate intake depends on what works best for you, at least in the short term.

For most people, 60 to 120 grams of carbohydrates is better than consuming less than 60 grams of carbs daily. Dr. DiNicolantonio does better on a moderate daily carbohydrate intake of around 120 to 150 grams. His energy levels and exercise capacity are better with a moderate carbohydrate intake versus a low carbohydrate intake. However, certain people do not tolerate fruits or vegetables and do better eating little to no carbohydrates. Thus, the answer to "What is the optimal amount of carbohydrates?" depends on your situation.

In the long term, it's better to consume some carbohydrates compared to none for several reasons:

- **Less ammonia production:** A higher carbohydrate intake lowers gluconeogenesis and the ammonia produced from breaking down amino acids to form glucose. The potassium citrate that's high in fruits also decreases ammonia production by offsetting the acid load and the negatively charged sulfate. Animal foods are higher in potassium chloride; thus, the potassium can't be as readily used to remove the negatively charged sulfate but instead follows the higher chloride.

- **Less stress hormone production immediately and less adrenal burnout and muscle breakdown in the long term:** In the short term, low-carb, ketogenic, and carnivore diets can increase cortisol and adrenaline to increase the breakdown of amino acids to form glucose via gluconeogenesis. If someone isn't ingesting enough amino acids, the body will break down skeletal muscle to form glucose. Over a longer period, cortisol and adrenaline levels may decrease on these types of diets. However, the reduction may be because of adrenal burnout and possibly an upregulation of either receptor sites for these hormones or more efficient effects downstream once the body can no longer produce such high amounts.

There is still much we do not know about why elevated stress hormones can decrease after a while on low-salt or low-carb diets. Still, it would be a big assumption that it's simply a normalization, particularly when most people who stay on low-salt or low-carb diets have all the signs of adrenal burnout. In animal studies, a low-salt diet has been shown to lead to adrenal hypertrophy, which is the prerequisite to organ burnout. Additionally, many anecdotes and case reports of people not tolerating low-carb, ketogenic, or carnivore diets after several months exist, which supports the idea that the normalization of hormones after several months may not be a normalization at all but a burnout of the system, particularly the adrenal glands.

- **More carbon dioxide (CO_2) production:** You may think more CO_2 production is bad. However, you need CO_2 to oxygenate the skeletal muscle during intense exercise because CO_2 allows hemoglobin to release its oxygen molecules. Also, CO_2 acts as an antioxidant and vasodilator. Glucose oxidation produces 50 percent more CO_2 than fat oxidation, so consuming some carbohydrates is beneficial for providing the body with more CO_2.

- **Better T3 production, higher body temperature, and increased metabolic rate:** Consuming carbohydrates allows better conversion of T4 to the active thyroid hormone T3, which helps support a higher metabolic rate and body temperature. If you feel cold all the time, the reason could be that you aren't consuming enough carbohydrates.

- **Less elevation in fasting glucose:** Most people who go on a low-carb, ketogenic, or carnivore diet end up with an elevated fasting glucose level. Eventually, fasting blood sugar typically elevates, although it may take months or even years, likely due to the enhanced fatty acid oxidation and the greater amounts of fatty acids released from the adipocyte, which can lead to insulin resistance.

- **Less omega-6 oxidation production:** Greater amounts of omega-6 polyunsaturated oxidation products are released when you're in a chronic state of fat-burning because most people have a lot of omega-6 stores in their fat from decades of eating a diet high in omega-6 polyunsaturated fat.

Your brain needs about 130 grams of glucose to function, plus you need more for your eyes and red blood cells, which also run on glucose. Being in a state of full ketosis may reduce your need for glucose by up to 45 percent, but your brain still needs 71.5 grams of glucose. Dietary fat contributes only a little to gluconeogenesis. Ninety-five percent of dietary fat is triglycerides, and only 5 percent of triglycerides are converted to glucose; 10 percent of triglycerides is glycerol, and it takes two glycerol molecules to form glucose. Consequently, consuming even as much as 160 grams of dietary fat provides only 7.5 to 8 grams of glucose. It has been said that fat-burning in prolonged fasting may contribute up to 20 percent of the glucose needed for gluconeogenesis. So, even if we assume that a ketogenic or carnivore diet provides fat-burning similar to prolonged fasting (which it doesn't), 20 percent of 130 grams of glucose is 26 grams. Thus, you still need 38 grams or more of glucose to power your brain.

The efficiency of amino acids to form glucose is only about 50 percent. Thus, at least 75 grams of protein are needed to provide the 38 or so grams of glucose to meet the brain's needs. For someone eating 150 grams of protein on a ketogenic or carnivore diet, half of their protein intake (75 grams) will go toward gluconeogenesis instead of muscle protein synthesis or amino acid recycling. That's a big protein deficit, which could make it difficult to gain muscle or may potentially even lead to muscle loss. In other words, it would take a consistently high protein intake for a zero-carb diet not to cause issues of muscle loss, and that means a greater acid load and all the other harms that come from eating high dietary acid loads.

If you tolerate carbohydrates, the general guideline is that your intake can go up as your activity level increases. So, if you are inactive, you may be able to get away with eating only 60 grams of carbohydrates per day. However, if you are moderately active (weight training two or three times per week and doing cardio two or three times per week), you may do better consuming 120 grams per day or more.

Very active people can get away with eating even more carbohydrates—30 to 40 percent of total calories from carbs per day—but for most people, consuming around 15 to 20 percent of total calories as carbohydrates seems better for overall health. The typical upper level for carbohydrate intake for most people who are somewhat active is 150 to 200 grams per day. Once you start increasing daily total carbohydrate intake to more than 150 to 200 grams, activity levels must increase substantially to offset blood sugar and insulin spikes. In other words, match your carbohydrate intake to your activity level.

What types of carbohydrates should you eat?

You should minimize your consumption of carbohydrates that provide little to no nutrition, don't curb hunger, and are highly processed. Examples include added sugars (table sugar and high-fructose corn syrup), refined carbohydrates (cereals, bread, and pasta), and rice. Yes, rice is nutrient poor, is not very satiating, and spikes blood glucose. We're not saying you can't integrate rice into your diet in small quantities, but you shouldn't overconsume it, and eating potatoes or fruit is a much better option. If you do have rice, make sure to have it after you eat protein, which can lower the blood sugar spike.

Why you need more salt on a low-carbohydrate diet

The first one to two weeks on a low-carbohydrate diet causes sodium loss because insulin levels drop, and the kidneys spill sodium in the urine. The "keto flu" people experience during the first couple of weeks is the result. After that initial period, sodium loss decreases, but you still need more salt because carbohydrates help absorb dietary sodium. Thus, when you're on a low-carb diet, your body doesn't absorb sodium as well, and you need more salt. That's another reason so many people feel better when they continue to add salt to their high-animal-protein diet.

MAKING THE *Best* FOOD CHOICES

What types of animal proteins should you consume?

The best meat to consume is 100 percent grass-fed beef, bison, elk, venison, and lamb. Grass-fed meat is leaner, contains more protein, and has less fat than grain-fed meat. Pasture-raised pork, which comes from pigs that eat off the land and are set to pasture, is also fine to consume. However, most pork is not pasture raised, so read labels carefully or source your pork from a local farm that is transparent about its practices. We prefer Iberico pork because it contains more oleic acid, and the acorns in its diet give the meat a nice, almost nutty flavor. However, any pastured heritage breed of pork will give you higher-quality meat than conventional factory-farmed pork.

Ideally, you want to eat pasture-raised chicken, where the chickens are set to pasture and eat worms, grubs, and insects. Organic chicken is the next best thing if you can't afford or find pasture-raised chicken.

The best eggs come from pasture-raised hens. Cage-free or organic eggs are a step up from conventional eggs but are not optimal. Pasture-raised eggs have more vitamins, minerals, and antioxidants, which help keep the omega-6 in the yolks from oxidizing.

For seafood, it's important to eat wild fish or fish primarily fed things like krill feed. Consuming farm-raised fish can be okay as long as the feed and their living conditions are high quality. Norway produces some very good farm-raised fish, but it's best to avoid farm-raised fish from the United States unless you can confirm that the quality of the feed and the living conditions are good.

Dairy is important for calcium but should come from 100 percent grass-fed cows. If you eat non-grass-fed dairy, ensure it's low fat or no fat because the fat is where all the pesticides and other harmful fat-soluble pollutants in grain feed can accumulate.

What kinds of plant foods should you consume?

Ideally, you should choose organic plant foods you tolerate (meaning you don't have bloating, gas, upset stomach, and so on), limiting the high-oxalate produce and nuts discussed earlier. Dr. DiNicolantonio enjoys organic peaches, nectarines, blueberries, and strawberries.

If organic produce is beyond your budget or otherwise unavailable, minimize eating what the Environmental Working Group identifies as the "Dirty Dozen" because they have thin skins and are typically sprayed with a lot of pesticides. The most recent list includes strawberries, spinach, kale, mustard and collard greens, peaches, pears, nectarines, apples, grapes, bell and hot peppers, cherries, blueberries, and green beans.

Another option is to soak the fruit or vegetables in a mixture of approximately 1 teaspoon of bicarbonate powder (Dr. DiNicolantonio opens up the sodium/potassium bicarbonate capsules) per liter of water for 15 minutes. This process can help remove a lot of the pesticides.

What types of oils and fats should you consume, and which should you avoid?

The best fats and oils to consume include 100 percent grass-fed butter, coconut oil, extra-virgin olive oil, and avocado oil. Ghee, tallow, and cultured oil are also excellent choices, although we don't use them in the recipes in this book. Cultured oil is made similarly to how cows turn grass into fats, but the process uses microbial fermentation of grass. The oil contains more than 90 percent monounsaturated fat, but it uses much less water to produce than the production of olive oil does.

Avoid cooking with industrial seed oils, such as corn, soybean, canola, cottonseed, safflower, sunflower, rice bran, and grapeseed. A little bit of cold-pressed sunflower oil poured on a salad may be fine, but utilizing high heat/hexane-extracted industrial seed oils is unhealthy. These oils are already oxidized before they're cooked. Once cooked, their oxidation products increase dramatically because seed oils are polyunsaturated fats with many double bonds susceptible to free radical attack. Additionally, when you consume these seed oils, your stomach acid further oxidizes the omega-6 to hydroperoxides and aldehydes, which are harmful and carcinogenic.

Most people do best when they get 25 to 35 percent of their total calories from dietary fat. Low-fat diets, particularly those in which fat provides less than 15 percent of total calories, are almost impossible to sustain in the long run. You need a certain amount of fat to live, and you need fat to thrive. Dietary fat provides energy and satiety, and it improves hormone production. Additionally, when you lower fat too much, typically carbohydrates have to replace it, and people can easily get into trouble if their carbohydrate intake goes even slightly higher than they need.

Ultimately, most of your dietary fat should come from whole foods, particularly grass-fed dairy, but you can also get some fat from grass-fed meat, eggs, and perhaps a small amount of nuts, if tolerated.

REFERENCES

1. Ben-Dor, M., et al., Man the fat hunter: the demise of Homo erectus and the emergence of a new hominin lineage in the Middle Pleistocene (ca. 400 kyr) Levant. *PLoS One*, 2011. 6(12): p. e28689.

2. Neuhauser, B., et al., Coffee consumption and total body water homeostasis as measured by fluid balance and bioelectrical impedance analysis. *Ann Nutr Metab*, 1997. 41(1): p. 29-36.

3. DiNicolantonio, J. J. and J. H. O'Keefe, Sodium restriction and insulin resistance: a review of 23 clinical trials. *J Metab Health*. 2022. 6(1): p. a78.

4. Nishimuta, M., et al., Dietary salt (sodium chloride) requirement and adverse effects of salt restriction in humans. *J Nutr Sci Vitaminol* (Tokyo), 2018. 64(2): p. 83-89.

5. Xavier, A. R., et al., Dietary sodium restriction exacerbates age-related changes in rat adipose tissue and liver lipogenesis. *Metabolism*, 2003. 52(8): p. 1072-7.

6. Rodriguez, N. R., Introduction to protein summit 2.0: continued exploration of the impact of high-quality protein on optimal health. *Am J Clin Nutr*, 2015. 101(6): p. 1317s-1319s.

7. DiNicolantonio, J. J. and J. O'Keefe, Low-grade metabolic acidosis as a driver of chronic disease: a 21st century public health crisis. *Open Heart*, 2021. 8(2): p. e001730.

8. Ibid.

9. Lennon, E. J. and J. Lemann, Jr., Influence of diet composition on endogenous fixed acid production. *Am J Clin Nutr*, 1968. 21(5): p. 451-6.

10. Lennon, E. J., J. Lemann, Jr., and J. R. Litzow, The effects of diet and stool composition on the net external acid balance of normal subjects. *J Clin Invest*, 1966. 45(10): p. 1601-7.

11. McClellan, W. S. and E. F. Bois, Clinical calorimetry xlv. Prolonged meat diets with a study of kidney function and ketosis. *J Biol Chem*. 1930. 87: p. 651-68.

12. Reddy, S. T., et al., Effect of low-carbohydrate high-protein diets on acid-base balance, stone-forming propensity, and calcium metabolism. *Am J Kidney Dis*, 2002. 40(2): p. 265-74.

13. Adams, N. D., R. W. Gray, and J. Lemann, Jr., The calciuria of increased fixed acid production in humans: evidence against a role for parathyroid hormone and 1,25(OH)2-vitamin D. *Calcif Tissue Int*, 1979. 28(3): p. 233-8.

14. Chu, J. Y., S. Margen, and F. M. Costa, Studies in calcium metabolism. II. Effects of low calcium and variable protein intake on human calcium metabolism. *Am J Clin Nutr*, 1975. 28(9): p. 1028-35.

15. Lutz, J., Calcium balance and acid-base status of women as affected by increased protein intake and by sodium bicarbonate ingestion. *Am J Clin Nutr*, 1984. 39(2): p. 281-8.

16. Buclin, T., et al., Diet acids and alkalis influence calcium retention in bone. *Osteoporos Int*, 2001. 12(6): p. 493-9.

17. Kerstetter, J. E., et al., Changes in bone turnover in young women consuming different levels of dietary protein. *J Clin Endocrinol Metab*, 1999. 84(3): p. 1052-5.

18. Breslau, N. A., et al., Relationship of animal protein-rich diet to kidney stone formation and calcium metabolism. *J Clin Endocrinol Metab*, 1988. 66(1): p. 140-6.

19. Lemann, J., Jr., J. R. Litzow, and E. J. Lennon, The effects of chronic acid loads in normal man: further evidence for the participation of bone mineral in the defense against chronic metabolic acidosis. *J Clin Invest*, 1966. 45(10): p. 1608-14.

20. Kurtz, I., et al., Effect of diet on plasma acid-base composition in normal humans. *Kidney Int*, 1983. 24(5): p. 670-80.

21. Marunaka, Y., The proposal of molecular mechanisms of weak organic acids intake-induced improvement of insulin resistance in diabetes mellitus via elevation of interstitial fluid pH. *Int J Mol Sci*, 2018. 19(10).

22. Vormann, J., et al., Supplementation with alkaline minerals reduces symptoms in patients with chronic low back pain. *J Trace Elem Med Biol*, 2001. 15(2-3): p. 179-83.

23. Weigle, D. S., et al., A high-protein diet induces sustained reductions in appetite, ad libitum caloric intake, and body weight despite compensatory changes in diurnal plasma leptin and ghrelin concentrations. *Am J Clin Nutr*, 2005. 82(1): p. 41-8.

24. Bray, G. A., et al., Effect of protein overfeeding on energy expenditure measured in a metabolic chamber. *Am J Clin Nutr*, 2015. 101(3): p. 496-505.

25. Crovetti, R., et al., The influence of thermic effect of food on satiety. *Eur J Clin Nutr*, 1998. 52(7): p. 482-8.

26. Cirillo, M., et al., Effects of a meat meal on renal sodium handling and sodium balance. *Miner Electrolyte Metab*, 1998. 24(4): p. 279-84.

RECIPES

BREAKFASTS

HIGH-PROTEIN SMOOTHIE—FOUR WAYS

YIELD: 1 serving
PREP TIME: 5 minutes

1. Put all the ingredients in a blender.
2. Blend on high speed until smooth and creamy. Enjoy immediately.

Raspberry Tahini Smoothie

Most often, tahini is used in savory preparations, like hummus. But it works just as well in fruit smoothies as a replacement for your favorite nut butter. Try experimenting with the way tahini can interact with different flavors and substitute blackberries or strawberries for the raspberries.

1 cup ice

½ cup raspberries, fresh or frozen

½ banana

1 tablespoon tahini

¼ teaspoon ground cinnamon

Pinch of Redmond Real Salt

1 scoop vanilla whey protein powder

1 cup whole milk

CALORIES 446 | **PROTEIN** 37g | **CARBS** 40.5g | **SUGARS** 23.8g | **FIBER** 8.2g | **FAT** 18.1g

Vanilla Fig Almond Smoothie

Fig and almond are classic ingredients in Spanish cuisine. Enjoy this powerhouse combination of flavors in your morning smoothie.

1 cup ice

¼ cup plain Greek yogurt (5% fat)

⅓ banana

4 fresh black Mission figs

1 tablespoon raw almond butter

1 scoop vanilla whey protein powder

1 cup water

CALORIES 446 | **PROTEIN** 37g | **CARBS** 40.5g | **SUGARS** 23.8g | **FIBER** 8.2g | **FAT** 18.1g

Chocolate Almond Butter Cup Smoothie

Reminiscent of a beloved childhood candy! Give this smoothie a textured garnish by topping it with 1 tablespoon of sliced almonds and ½ teaspoon of raw cacao nibs and eat it with a spoon.

1 cup ice

⅓ banana

1 tablespoon raw almond butter

1 teaspoon chia seeds

1 scoop chocolate whey protein powder

1 cup whole milk

CALORIES 423 | **PROTEIN** 34.4g | **CARBS** 29g | **SUGARS** 19.8g | **FIBER** 5.1g | **FAT** 20.2g

Green Avocado Smoothie

Best to get your greens in first thing. The chia seeds in this smoothie can help you feel fuller longer. You can experiment with different greens in place of the kale. If you like a more bitter peppery flavor, for example, try arugula.

1 cup ice

½ small ripe avocado

½ cup chopped curly kale leaves, stemmed

1 teaspoon chia seeds

1 scoop vanilla whey protein powder

1 cup water

CALORIES 227 | **PROTEIN** 26.5g | **CARBS** 9.8g | **SUGARS** 2.5g | **FIBER** 6.6g | **FAT** 10.6g

LEMON CHIA

YIELD: 12 muffins (2 per serving) | **PREP TIME:** 12 minutes | **COOK TIME:** 20 minutes

This is a high-protein makeover of the classic lemon poppy seed muffin. Add 1 cup of fresh or frozen blueberries to the batter before baking to make blueberry lemon muffins.

2 cups gluten-free oat flour

⅓ cup unflavored whey protein powder

2 tablespoons chia seeds

2 teaspoons baking powder

¼ teaspoon baking soda

¼ teaspoon Redmond Real Salt

3 large eggs

1 cup plain Greek yogurt (5% fat)

¾ cup maple syrup

Grated zest of 2 lemons

¼ cup lemon juice

1 teaspoon vanilla extract

½ cup (1 stick) unsalted butter, melted and cooled

½ teaspoon white miso paste

1. Preheat the oven to 375°F.
2. Whisk together the oat flour, whey protein, chia seeds, baking powder, baking soda, and salt in a medium bowl.
3. Put the eggs, yogurt, maple syrup, lemon zest, lemon juice, vanilla, butter, and miso in a stand mixer fitted with the paddle attachment. Beat on medium speed until smooth and creamy. Add the flour mixture and mix on low speed until thoroughly combined.
4. Spoon the batter into a standard-size, 12-well nonstick muffin pan, filling the wells three-quarters of the way full.
5. Bake for 20 minutes, or until a toothpick inserted into a muffin comes out clean.
6. Let cool slightly before removing from the pan. Store in an airtight container in the refrigerator for up to 3 days or in the freezer for up to 3 months.

PER SERVING:
CALORIES 524 | **PROTEIN** 14g | **CARBS** 64g | **SUGARS** 36g | **FIBER** 4g | **FAT** 23g

CHOCOLATE CHIP WALNUT *Muffins*

YIELD: 12 muffins (2 per serving) | **PREP TIME:** 12 minutes | **COOK TIME:** 20 minutes

The yogurt in this recipe helps keep these muffins super moist. Want a burst of fruit? Try adding 1 cup of fresh or frozen raspberries to the batter.

2 cups gluten-free oat flour

2 teaspoons baking powder

½ teaspoon Redmond Real Salt

1 cup plain Greek yogurt (5% fat)

½ cup (1 stick) unsalted butter, melted and cooled

1 teaspoon vanilla extract

1 cup maple syrup

3 large eggs

¼ cup chopped dark chocolate

¼ cup chopped raw walnuts

1. Preheat the oven to 350°F.
2. Whisk together the flour, baking powder, and salt in a medium bowl.
3. Put the yogurt, butter, vanilla, maple syrup, and eggs in a stand mixer fitted with the paddle attachment. Beat on medium speed until smooth and creamy. Add the flour mixture and mix on low speed until thoroughly combined. Stir in the chocolate and walnuts.
4. Spoon the batter into a standard-size, 12-well nonstick muffin pan, filling the wells three-quarters of the way full.
5. Bake for 20 minutes, or until a toothpick inserted into a muffin comes out clean.
6. Let cool slightly before removing from the pan. Once completely cool, store in an airtight container in the refrigerator for up to 3 days or in the freezer for up to 3 months.

PER SERVING:
CALORIES 546 | **PROTEIN** 10g | **CARBS** 66g | **SUGARS** 38g | **FIBER** 4g | **FAT** 27g

CHOCOLATE BLISS
Breakfast Loaf

YIELD: 12 slices (1 or 2 per serving) | **PREP TIME:** 12 minutes | **COOK TIME:** 40 minutes

Two slices of this loaf are great for breakfast, or enjoy one slice as an on-the-go afternoon snack. For breakfast, top the slices with 2 tablespoons of Greek yogurt and ½ cup of raspberries or sliced strawberries.

- 1½ cups brown rice flour
- ½ cup hazelnut flour
- ½ cup cacao powder
- 2 teaspoons baking powder
- Pinch of Redmond Real Salt
- 3 large eggs
- 1 cup plain Greek yogurt (5% fat)
- 1 cup maple syrup
- 1 teaspoon vanilla extract
- 1 teaspoon red miso paste
- ½ cup (1 stick) unsalted butter, melted and cooled
- 1 tablespoon cacao nibs

1. Preheat the oven to 350°F.
2. Whisk together the rice flour, hazelnut flour, cacao powder, baking powder, and salt in a medium bowl. Set aside.
3. Put the eggs, yogurt, maple syrup, vanilla, miso, and butter in a stand mixer fitted with the paddle attachment. Beat on medium speed until smooth and creamy. Add the flour mixture and mix on low speed until thoroughly combined.
4. Spoon the batter evenly into a 9 by 5-inch (1¼-pound) nonstick loaf pan. Sprinkle the cacao nibs on top.
5. Bake for 40 minutes, or until a toothpick inserted into the center of the loaf comes out clean.
6. Let cool slightly before removing from the pan. Allow to cool fully before slicing. Store in an airtight container in the refrigerator for up to 5 days or in the freezer for up to 3 months.

PER SLICE:
CALORIES 259 | **PROTEIN** 4.8g | **CARBS** 34g | **SUGARS** 17.8g | **FIBER** 2.3g | **FAT** 12.6g

INDIVIDUAL GREEK YOGURT *Cheesecakes*

YIELD: 9 small cheesecakes (1 per serving) | **PREP TIME:** 15 minutes | **COOK TIME:** 30 minutes

You can enjoy these cheesecakes for breakfast, dessert, or an afternoon snack. They're best when chilled. Want to add more fiber to this dish? Top it with fresh blueberries or sliced black Mission figs.

GRANOLA CRUST:

¾ cup gluten-free rolled oats

¼ cup chopped pecans

2 tablespoons extra-virgin coconut oil, melted and cooled

2 tablespoons honey

½ teaspoon ground cinnamon

Pinch of Redmond Real Salt

FILLING:

16 ounces cream cheese, room temperature

1 cup plain Greek yogurt (5% fat)

¼ cup honey

1 large egg

2 teaspoons tapioca starch

1 teaspoon vanilla extract

¼ teaspoon grated lemon zest

Pinch of fresh grated nutmeg

1. Preheat the oven to 325°F.
2. Line nine wells of a standard-size muffin pan with paper muffin cups. Set aside.
3. Make the crust: Combine the oats, pecans, coconut oil, honey, cinnamon, and salt in a medium bowl. Divide the granola mixture evenly among the lined muffin cups. Press down firmly to make a bottom crust. Set aside.
4. Make the filling: Put the cream cheese, yogurt, honey, egg, tapioca starch, vanilla, lemon zest, and nutmeg in a stand mixer fitted with the paddle attachment. Beat until smooth and creamy. Spoon into the muffin cups, filling each well about two-thirds full.
5. Bake for 30 minutes, or until set. Let cool completely before removing from the pan. If desired, chill the cakes before serving. Store in an airtight container in the refrigerator for up to 5 days or in the freezer for up to 3 months.

PER CHEESECAKE:
CALORIES 298 | **PROTEIN** 6g | **CARBS** 19.9g | **SUGARS** 14.6g | **FIBER** 1g | **FAT** 22.6g

WHEY

YIELD: 6 large waffles (1 per serving) | **PREP TIME:** 10 minutes | **COOK TIME:** 15 minutes

This is a great make-ahead recipe. You can freeze these waffles and have toaster waffles all week long. Experiment with different toppings, like yogurt and berries or apple, nut butter, and cinnamon.

2 cups gluten-free oat flour

¼ cup unflavored whey protein powder

1 tablespoon baking powder

½ teaspoon ground cinnamon

¼ teaspoon Redmond Real Salt

1¼ cups whole milk

½ cup plain Greek yogurt (5% fat)

¼ cup (½ stick) unsalted butter, melted and cooled

2 tablespoons maple syrup

2 large eggs

1 teaspoon vanilla extract

1. Preheat a waffle iron according to the manufacturer's instructions.
2. Whisk together the oat flour, whey protein, baking powder, cinnamon, and salt in a medium bowl. Set aside.
3. Put the milk, yogurt, butter, maple syrup, eggs, and vanilla in a stand mixer fitted with the paddle attachment. Beat on medium speed until smooth. Add the flour mixture and mix on low speed until thoroughly combined.
4. Ladle one-sixth of the batter into the waffle iron. Following the manufacturer's guidelines, cook until golden and crisp. Repeat with the remaining batter, making a total of six waffles.
5. Store in an airtight container in the refrigerator for up to 3 days or in the freezer for up to 3 months.

PER WAFFLE:
CALORIES 320 | **PROTEIN** 13.4g | **CARBS** 32.4g | **SUGARS** 8g | **FIBER** 2.8g | **FAT** 14.3g

EVERYTHING *Bagels*

YIELD: 10 bagels (1 per serving) | **PREP TIME:** 6 minutes (not including time to make salt rub) | **COOK TIME:** 20 minutes

Say goodbye to gluten and hello to protein with this bagel makeover. We love to spread them with cream cheese and pile on wild-caught smoked salmon and scallions. You can play around with different flavor combinations. For cinnamon raisin bagels, add ½ teaspoon of ground cinnamon and ½ cup of raisins to the batter and omit the salt rub.

- 1¾ cups egg whites (see note)
- 1 cup gluten-free oat flour
- ¼ cup psyllium husks
- ¾ cup unflavored whey protein powder
- 2 teaspoons baking powder
- ¼ teaspoon Redmond Real Salt
- 3 tablespoons Everything Bagel Salt Rub (page 223)

Special equipment:

Two 6-well nonstick donut pans

1. Preheat the oven to 325°F.
2. Whisk together the egg whites, flour, psyllium, whey protein, baking powder, and salt in a medium bowl.
3. Spoon the batter evenly into ten wells of the donut pans. Sprinkle with the salt rub.
4. Bake for 20 minutes, or until a toothpick inserted into a bagel comes out clean.
5. Let cool completely before removing from the pan. Store in an airtight container in the refrigerator for up to 3 days.

Note: For this quantity of egg whites, you'll need 14 to 17 large eggs. You can also buy a carton of egg whites for this purpose.

PER BAGEL:
CALORIES 119 | **PROTEIN** 13.7g | **CARBS** 11.1g | **SUGARS** 0.6g | **FIBER** 3.1g | **FAT** 1.5g

COTTAGE CHEESE *Egg Scramble*

YIELD: 2 servings | **PREP TIME:** 2 minutes | **COOK TIME:** 2 minutes

The egg-and-cheese protein combo makes this a super filling breakfast and a great way to start the day. Try pairing it with your favorite sautéed greens and some tomatoes.

6 large eggs

¾ cup cottage cheese (full fat)

¼ teaspoon Redmond Real Salt

2 teaspoons extra-virgin olive oil

2 teaspoons chopped fresh chives, for garnish

1. Whisk together the eggs, cottage cheese, and salt in a medium bowl.
2. Heat a medium nonstick skillet over medium heat, then pour in the olive oil. Add the egg mixture and spread it to coat the pan. Pull the eggs across the pan with a rubber spatula and continue stirring until the eggs start to set, 1½ to 2 minutes.
3. Garnish with the chives and enjoy immediately.

PER SERVING:
CALORIES 326 | **PROTEIN** 28.6g | **CARBS** 4.7g | **SUGARS** 3.8g | **FIBER** 0.1g | **FAT** 21g

DENVER-STYLE *Frittata*

YIELD: 2 servings | **PREP TIME:** 12 minutes | **COOK TIME:** 30 minutes

The yogurt in this recipe gives the frittata a light and creamy texture and ups the protein content. You can add ¾ cup of diced cooked sweet potatoes or white potatoes for a denser frittata.

5 large eggs

½ cup plain Greek yogurt (5% fat)

¼ teaspoon Redmond Real Salt

Pinch of ground nutmeg

1 tablespoon extra-virgin olive oil

⅓ cup chopped yellow onions

⅓ cup chopped green bell peppers

⅓ cup chopped red bell peppers

¾ cup diced cooked ham

½ cup shredded cheddar cheese

1. Preheat the oven to 325°F.
2. Whisk together the eggs, yogurt, salt, and nutmeg in a medium bowl. Set aside.
3. Heat a medium nonstick ovenproof skillet over medium heat, then pour in the olive oil. Add the onions and bell peppers and sauté until softened, about 4 minutes. Stir in the ham. Pour in the egg mixture and spread evenly in the pan. Top with the cheese.
4. Bake for 25 minutes, or until the cheese is melted and the eggs are set in the center. Allow to cool slightly before serving.

PER SERVING:
CALORIES 455 | **PROTEIN** 34.5g | **CARBS** 10.9g | **SUGARS** 5.7g | **FIBER** 1g | **FAT** 32.1g

CAULIFLOWER BACON *Frittata*

YIELD: 2 servings | **PREP TIME:** 16 minutes | **COOK TIME:** 38 minutes

This frittata combines layers of savory flavors that easily translate to a lunch meal with an arugula salad. You can add ¾ cup of diced cooked sweet potatoes or white potatoes for a denser frittata.

4 ounces bacon, cut crosswise into ¼-inch strips

6 large eggs

⅓ cup grated Parmesan cheese

2 tablespoons chopped fresh Italian parsley

¼ teaspoon Redmond Real Salt

2 tablespoons extra-virgin olive oil

2 cups cauliflower florets

2 cloves garlic, minced

1. Preheat the oven to 325°F.
2. Cook the bacon in a medium nonstick ovenproof skillet over medium heat until crisp. Remove the bacon from the pan, pour off the fat, and allow the bacon to cool.
3. Whisk together the eggs, Parmesan, parsley, and salt in a medium bowl. Add the cooled bacon. Set aside.
4. Using the same skillet, heat the olive oil over medium heat. Add the cauliflower and cook, stirring occasionally, until golden brown, about 12 minutes. Add the garlic and continue cooking for 1 minute, stirring constantly. Pour in the egg mixture.
5. Bake for 20 minutes, or until the center of the frittata is set. Allow to cool slightly before serving.

PER SERVING:

CALORIES 696 | **PROTEIN** 44.3g | **CARBS** 9g | **SUGARS** 3.3g | **FIBER** 2.2g | **FAT** 55.3g

SOUTHWEST

YIELD: 12 egg cups (2 per serving) | **PREP TIME:** 16 minutes | **COOK TIME:** 30 minutes

This is a terrific recipe to bake ahead on a Sunday so you have egg cups for breakfasts and snacks all week. You can dress them up for a Sunday brunch by adding tomato salsa and avocado slices as accompaniments.

12 large eggs

1 teaspoon Redmond Real Salt, divided

2 tablespoons avocado oil

¾ cup chopped green bell peppers

¾ cup chopped red bell peppers

½ cup diced red onions

8 ounces ground turkey (85% lean)

1½ teaspoons ground cumin

1 teaspoon ground coriander

½ teaspoon smoked paprika

1 cup shredded cheddar cheese

1. Preheat the oven to 325°F.
2. Whisk together the eggs and ½ teaspoon of the salt in a large bowl. Set aside.
3. Heat a large skillet over medium heat, then pour in the avocado oil. Add the bell peppers and onions and cook until soft, about 4 minutes.
4. Add the ground turkey, remaining ½ teaspoon of salt, cumin, coriander, and paprika. Cook, stirring the turkey to break up the clumps, until it is fully browned, about 5 minutes. Remove from the heat and allow to cool slightly.
5. Pour the eggs evenly into a standard-size, 12-well nonstick muffin pan, filling the wells about two-thirds full. Spoon in the turkey mixture, using 2 tablespoons per muffin well. Sprinkle the cheese evenly on top.
6. Bake for 20 minutes, or until the eggs are set in the center. Allow to cool slightly.
7. Use a small offset spatula to scrape around the muffin wells to release the egg cups. Store leftovers in an airtight container in the refrigerator for up to 3 days or in the freezer for up to 3 months. Enjoy cold or reheat in an oven at 375°F for 6 minutes.

PER SERVING:

CALORIES 310 | **PROTEIN** 21.9g | **CARBS** 5.3g | **SUGARS** 3.2g | **FIBER** 1.1g | **FAT** 23.5g

SOUPS *and* BROTHS

GINGER TURMERIC CHICKEN *Bone Broth*

YIELD: 3 quarts (1 cup per serving) | **PREP TIME:** 15 minutes | **COOK TIME:** 4 hours

This broth is great on its own or as the foundation for just about any soup recipe. Play around with the flavor by adding ingredients like lemongrass and cilantro.

6 pounds chicken bones, preferably necks, backs, and feet

2 small yellow onions, rinsed well and quartered (leave peels on)

3 carrots, cut into 1-inch pieces

3 stalks celery, cut into 1-inch pieces

1 tablespoon grated fresh ginger

1 tablespoon grated fresh turmeric

1 head garlic, halved crosswise

1 bay leaf

1 teaspoon Redmond Real Salt

1 teaspoon black peppercorns

1 tablespoon apple cider vinegar

12 cups water

1. Rinse the chicken bones with cold water.
2. Put the bones, onions, carrots, celery, ginger, turmeric, garlic, bay leaf, salt, peppercorns, and vinegar in a 6-quart stockpot. Cover with the water.
3. Cover the pot, place over medium-high heat, and bring to a boil; this takes about 45 minutes.
4. Lower the heat to a simmer and continue to cook for 3 hours 15 minutes.
5. Strain the broth with a fine-mesh strainer and discard the solids and fat.
6. Serve immediately. Store in an airtight container in the refrigerator for up to 5 days or in the freezer for up to 3 months.

PER SERVING:
CALORIES 32 | **PROTEIN** 1.5g | **CARBS** 5.2g | **SUGARS** 1.9g | **FIBER** 1.2g | **FAT** 0.6g

GARLIC THYME BEEF Bone Broth

YIELD: 3 quarts (1 cup per serving) | **PREP TIME:** 15 minutes | **COOK TIME:** 4 hours

For a richer-tasting broth, you can simmer it for 12 hours. For a deeper flavor, add 2 tablespoons of tomato paste to the broth while it is simmering.

4 pounds beef bones (marrow, oxtail, and knuckle bones cut in half)

1 small yellow onion, quartered

1 leek, ends trimmed, cut into 1-inch pieces, and rinsed

3 carrots, cut into 1-inch pieces

3 stalks celery, cut into 1-inch pieces

1 head garlic, rinsed and halved crosswise

2 bay leaves

1 bunch fresh thyme

1 tablespoon black peppercorns

1 tablespoon apple cider vinegar

1 teaspoon Redmond Real Salt

12 cups water

1. Preheat the oven to 425°F.
2. Put the bones, onion, leek, carrots, and celery in a roasting pan. Roast until browned, about 20 minutes.
3. Transfer the roasted bones and vegetables to a 6-quart stockpot. Add the garlic, bay leaves, thyme, peppercorns, vinegar, and salt. Cover with the water.
4. Cover the pot with the lid. Bring the broth to a rolling boil over medium-high heat (takes about 45 minutes).
5. Lower the heat to a simmer and continue to cook for 3 hours 15 minutes.
6. Strain the broth with a fine-mesh strainer and discard the solids and fat.
7. Serve immediately. Store the soup in an airtight container in the refrigerator for up to 5 days or in the freezer for up to 3 months.

PER SERVING:
CALORIES 33 | PROTEIN 1.8g | CARBS 5.4g | SUGARS 1.6g | FIBER 1.4g | FAT 0.6g

HIGH-PROTEIN
Butternut Squash Soup

YIELD: 6 servings | **PREP TIME:** 15 minutes | **COOK TIME:** 45 minutes

Cottage cheese, traditionally thought of as a breakfast food, also works well in savory dishes. It's a great way to pack more protein into a plant-forward recipe. Try garnishing this soup with chopped Granny Smith apples and crushed walnuts.

1 tablespoon extra-virgin olive oil

1 shallot, chopped

3 cloves garlic, minced

1 large butternut squash (about 3 pounds), peeled, seeded, and cut into 2-inch cubes

3 Granny Smith apples, peeled, cored, and cut into 2-inch cubes

5 sprigs fresh thyme

4 fresh sage leaves

1 teaspoon Redmond Real Salt

¼ teaspoon fresh grated nutmeg

1 tablespoon honey

4 cups chicken or beef bone broth

¾ cup full-fat cottage cheese

1. Heat a 6-quart stockpot over medium heat, then pour in the olive oil. Add the shallot and garlic and cook for 90 seconds, until fragrant.
2. Add the squash, apples, thyme, and sage. Continue to cook, stirring occasionally, for about 6 minutes, or until tender.
3. Add the salt, nutmeg, honey, and broth. Cover the pot and allow to cook over low heat for 35 minutes.
4. Remove from the heat and let cool slightly.
5. Transfer the mixture to a blender with the cottage cheese. Blend on medium-high speed until smooth and creamy, about 2 minutes.
6. Serve immediately. Store in an airtight container in the refrigerator for up to 5 days or in the freezer for up to 3 months.

PER SERVING:
CALORIES 137 | **PROTEIN** 7g | **CARBS** 23.3g | **SUGARS** 12.5g | **FIBER** 3.7g | **FAT** 3.2g

CREAMY TOMATO *Soup*

YIELD: 6 servings | **PREP TIME:** 10 minutes | **COOK TIME:** 35 minutes

This high-protein soup is great for a quick lunch or an afternoon snack. Try garnishing it with a few torn basil leaves and some grated lemon zest.

- 1 tablespoon extra-virgin olive oil
- 1 large red onion, diced
- 2 large carrots, diced
- 2 large stalks celery, diced
- 5 cloves garlic, minced
- 2 tablespoons tomato paste
- 2 cups beef bone broth
- 5 cups canned diced tomatoes (about 1½ [28-ounce] cans)
- 6 large fresh basil leaves
- 1 teaspoon Redmond Real Salt
- 1 cup full-fat cottage cheese
- Cracked black pepper

1. Heat a 6-quart stockpot over medium heat, then pour in the olive oil. Add the onion, carrots, and celery. Cook for 4 minutes, stirring occasionally, until the onion is translucent.
2. Add the garlic and tomato paste and continue to cook for 90 seconds, or until fragrant.
3. Add the broth, tomatoes, basil, and salt.
4. Reduce the heat to medium-low and cook, uncovered, for 30 minutes. Remove from the heat and allow to cool slightly.
5. Discard the basil leaves.
6. Transfer the tomato mixture to a blender, add the cottage cheese, and blend until smooth and creamy, about 2 minutes.
7. Season to taste with black pepper.
8. Serve immediately. Store in an airtight container in the refrigerator for up to 5 days or in the freezer for up to 3 months.

PER SERVING:
CALORIES 111 | **PROTEIN** 8.1g | **CARBS** 14.8g | **SUGARS** 7g | **FIBER** 3.8g | **FAT** 3.3g

HIGH-PROTEIN *Green Gazpacho*

YIELD: 4 servings | **PREP TIME:** 15 minutes

This soup is a perfect way to pack in protein and fiber on a hot summer day. Serve with Greek yogurt. Garnish with lemon zest and chopped dill.

- 2 English cucumbers, seeded, cut into chunks
- 1½ cups plain Greek yogurt (5% fat)
- ¼ cup unflavored whey protein powder
- 1 ripe avocado, peeled and pitted
- ¼ teaspoon grated lemon zest
- Juice of 1 lemon
- 1 clove garlic, peeled
- 1 green bell pepper, roughly chopped
- 1 cup fresh spinach
- 1 tablespoon chopped fresh dill
- ½ teaspoon chopped fresh tarragon
- 1 small jalapeño pepper, deveined and seeded
- 2 tablespoons extra-virgin olive oil
- 1 teaspoon Redmond Real Salt
- Cracked black pepper

1. Put the cucumbers, yogurt, whey protein, avocado, lemon zest and juice, garlic, bell pepper, spinach, dill, tarragon, jalapeño, olive oil, and salt in a blender. Blend on medium speed until the mixture is chunky. Season with black pepper to taste.
2. Chill before serving. Store in an airtight container in the refrigerator for up to 3 days.

PER SERVING:
CALORIES 257 | **PROTEIN** 14.2g | **CARBS** 17g | **SUGARS** 8.3g | **FIBER** 5.9g | **FAT** 14.9g

SMOKY SWEET POTATO SOUP *with Tangy Yogurt*

YIELD: 6 servings | **PREP TIME:** 5 minutes | **COOK TIME:** 25 minutes

Try using Greek yogurt in any traditional place you would use sour cream. It's less calorie-dense and higher in protein. If you want to add a garnish to this soup, top it with a few fresh cilantro leaves and a sprinkle of toasted pumpkin seeds.

SOUP:

2 tablespoons unsalted butter

1 yellow onion, diced

2 cloves garlic, minced

2 pounds sweet potatoes, peeled and chopped into 1½-inch cubes

4 cups chicken bone broth

1½ teaspoons smoked paprika

½ teaspoon ground nutmeg

½ teaspoon Redmond Real Salt

¼ teaspoon ground coriander

¼ teaspoon ground cumin

YOGURT TOPPING:

¾ cup plain Greek yogurt (5% fat)

Grated zest of 1 lime

Juice of 1 lime

Pinch of Redmond Real Salt

Cracked black pepper to taste

1. Melt the butter in a 6-quart stockpot over medium heat. Add the onion and cook, stirring occasionally, until translucent, about 4 minutes.
2. Add the garlic, sweet potatoes, broth, paprika, nutmeg, salt, coriander, and cumin. Simmer over medium-low heat for 20 minutes, or until the potatoes are tender. Remove from the heat and allow to cool slightly.
3. While the soup is cooling, mix together the ingredients for the yogurt topping in a medium bowl. Set aside.
4. Transfer the soup to a blender and blend on high speed until smooth and creamy.
5. Serve with a dollop of the yogurt topping. Store in an airtight container in the refrigerator for up to 5 days or in the freezer for up to 3 months.

PER SERVING:
CALORIES 216 | **PROTEIN** 5.7g | **CARBS** 36.9g | **SUGARS** 8.5g | **FIBER** 5.1g | **FAT** 4.8g

RED CURRY CHICKEN
Lemongrass Soup

YIELD: 4 servings | **PREP TIME:** 8 minutes (not including time to cook chicken)
COOK TIME: 45 minutes

You can swap the chicken in this recipe for your favorite meat or fish. Beef, pork, and salmon are all good options. For a richer, creamy soup, add 1 cup of coconut milk.

- 1 stalk lemongrass
- 2 teaspoons grated fresh ginger
- 3 cups beef bone broth
- 2 cups chicken bone broth
- 2½ tablespoons tamari
- 2 tablespoons honey
- Grated zest of 1 lime
- Juice of 1 lime
- 1 tablespoon extra-virgin coconut oil
- 1 yellow onion, diced
- 4 cups cremini mushrooms, stemmed and sliced
- 1 tablespoon red curry paste
- 2 plum tomatoes, diced
- 6 cups chopped baby bok choy
- ½ teaspoon Redmond Real Salt
- 1 pound boneless, skinless chicken breasts, cooked and diced

1. Peel off the outer leaves of the lemongrass and discard them, and trim off the root end. Cut the stalk in half lengthwise and smash with the back of a knife to release the flavor. Roughly chop the lemongrass.
2. Put the lemongrass, ginger, beef broth, chicken broth, tamari, honey, and lime zest and juice in a 6-quart stockpot over medium-high heat. Bring to a rolling boil, then reduce the heat to low and simmer for 15 minutes.
3. Strain the broth into a large bowl; discard the solids.
4. Return the pot to the stove. Melt the coconut oil in the pot over medium heat. Add the onion and cook, stirring occasionally, until translucent, about 4 minutes. Add the mushrooms and cook for 6 more minutes, or until the mushrooms are soft.
5. Add the curry paste, tomatoes, bok choy, and salt and simmer for 5 minutes. Stir in the chicken and cook for an additional 2 minutes.
6. Serve immediately. Store in an airtight container in the refrigerator for up to 3 days or in the freezer for up to 3 months.

PER SERVING:
CALORIES 241 | **PROTEIN** 24.9g | **CARBS** 22g | **SUGARS** 13.9g | **FIBER** 4.2g | **FAT** 7.3g

CHICKEN *and* TURKEY

BUFFALO Chicken Salad Cups

YIELD: 2 servings | **PREP TIME:** 15 minutes (not including time to cook chicken and make sauce)

You can play around with different greens for this salad, like romaine lettuce, gem lettuce, or young collard greens. If you try collards, make sure to remove the stem and rib before turning the leaf into a wrap. Want to elevate this dish? Top it with crumbled blue cheese or drizzle with blue cheese dressing.

1 pound boneless, skinless chicken breasts, cooked and shredded

½ teaspoon Redmond Real Salt

½ cup finely diced celery

½ cup finely diced carrots

⅓ cup finely diced red onions

½ cup plain Greek yogurt (5% fat)

⅓ cup Buffalo Sauce (page 212)

1 tablespoon chopped fresh Italian parsley

1 teaspoon chopped fresh dill

¼ teaspoon grated lemon zest

6 butter lettuce leaves, for serving

Cracked black pepper, for garnish

1. Put the chicken in a medium bowl. Season with the salt.
2. Add the celery, carrots, and onions and mix well.
3. Stir in the yogurt and Buffalo sauce.
4. Add the parsley, dill, and lemon zest and toss to combine.
5. To serve, spoon the chicken into the lettuce leaves and garnish with pepper.

PER SERVING:
CALORIES 349 | **PROTEIN** 54.9g | **CARBS** 10.4g | **SUGARS** 4.6g | **FIBER** 2.3g | **FAT** 8.6g

CHICKEN

YIELD: 2 servings | **PREP TIME:** 20 minutes (not including time to cook rice noodles and chicken and make sauce) | **COOK TIME:** 7 minutes

This Pad Thai recipe replaces the traditional peanut butter with almond butter. If you have a nut allergy, you can omit the cashews and use tahini instead of almond butter in the sauce. You can also swap out the chicken for your favorite protein (shrimp, beef, and pork are good choices).

1½ tablespoons avocado oil

½ small red onion, thinly sliced

1 small red bell pepper, thinly sliced

1 yellow bell pepper, thinly sliced

¼ teaspoon Redmond Real Salt

1 carrot, spiral sliced

1 zucchini, spiral sliced

4 ounces brown rice noodles, cooked according to package instructions

¼ cup Ginger Miso Almond Butter Sauce (page 208)

1 pound boneless, skinless chicken breasts, cooked and diced

FOR GARNISH:

¼ cup fresh cilantro leaves

¼ cup raw cashews

1 teaspoon of mixed black and white sesame seeds

Special equipment:

Spiral slicer

1. Heat a large skillet over medium heat. Pour in the avocado oil and swirl to coat the bottom of the pan.
2. Add the onion and bell peppers and season with the salt. Cook, stirring occasionally, until tender, about 4 minutes.
3. Add the carrot and zucchini "noodles." Continue cooking for an additional 3 minutes, stirring occasionally, until tender. Remove from the heat and allow to cool.
4. Put the rice noodles in a medium bowl. Add the vegetable mixture and sauce and mix well.
5. To serve, top the vegetables with the chicken, then garnish with the cilantro, cashews, and sesame seeds.

PER SERVING:

CALORIES 722 | **PROTEIN** 59.3g | **CARBS** 83.4g | **SUGARS** 14.5g | **FIBER** 8.3g | **FAT** 25.2g

CHICKEN Parm

YIELD: 4 servings | **PREP TIME:** 12 minutes | **COOK TIME:** 16 minutes

Quinoa flakes are a great substitute for panko or any type of breadcrumb. We like to serve this dish with Sautéed Rainbow Chard & Stems (page 175).

2 boneless, skinless chicken breasts (about 14 ounces)

½ teaspoon Redmond Real Salt

½ cup quinoa flakes

¼ cup golden flax meal

¼ cup gluten-free oat flour

1 large egg

3 tablespoons avocado oil

⅔ cup no-sugar-added tomato sauce

4 ounces fresh mozzarella cheese, sliced

Fresh basil leaves, for garnish

1. Preheat the oven to 400°F.
2. Slice the chicken breasts horizontally into two even pieces, then pound them until they are ½ inch thick. Season with the salt.
3. Mix the quinoa flakes and flax meal in a medium shallow bowl. Put the oat flour in another shallow bowl. In a third shallow bowl, beat the egg.
4. Dredge the chicken in the oat flour, coating it evenly; shake off any excess flour. Then dredge the chicken in the beaten egg and then the quinoa-flax mixture, again coating the chicken evenly and shaking off any excess.
5. Heat the avocado oil in a large cast-iron skillet over medium-high heat. Working in two batches, sear the chicken breasts until golden brown on both sides, about 2 minutes per side.
6. Transfer the skillet to the oven and bake for 10 minutes, or until golden brown.
7. Spoon the tomato sauce over the chicken and top with the mozzarella slices. Return the pan to the oven and bake for another 2 minutes, or until the cheese is melted.
8. Garnish with the basil and serve.

PER SERVING:
CALORIES 425 | **PROTEIN** 35.3g | **CARBS** 15.8g | **SUGARS** 2.3g | **FIBER** 7.63.8g | **FAT** 24.2g

AIR-FRIED CHICKEN WINGS
with Japanese-Style BBQ Sauce

YIELD: 2 servings | **PREP TIME:** 6 minutes (not including time to make sauce)
COOK TIME: 22 minutes

Wings are not just for football season—you can enjoy these wings all year round. Gnawing on chicken wings is a great way to get in some collagen, and using Japanese-Style BBQ Sauce allows you to change things up from the traditional wing flavor. If you prefer a more traditional wing, swap in the Buffalo Sauce on page 212.

1 pound chicken wings (drumettes only preferred)

1 teaspoon Redmond Real Salt

½ teaspoon garlic powder

½ teaspoon onion powder

¼ teaspoon paprika

1 tablespoon avocado oil

½ cup Japanese-Style BBQ Sauce (page 210)

FOR GARNISH (OPTIONAL):

2 tablespoons of chopped scallions

1 teaspoon of mixed black and white sesame seeds

1. Preheat an air fryer to 400°F. Line the air fryer tray with parchment paper.
2. Put the chicken wings in a medium bowl and toss with the salt, garlic powder, onion powder, paprika, and avocado oil.
3. Arrange a single layer of wings on the prepared tray. Make sure they are not touching.
4. Air-fry for 20 minutes, or according to the manufacturer's instructions for chicken wings.
5. Remove the wings from the air fryer and toss in a clean bowl with the BBQ sauce, coating them evenly.
6. Return the wings to the air fryer and cook for an additional 2 minutes, until crispy. Serve immediately.

PER SERVING:
CALORIES 568 | **PROTEIN** 32.7g | **CARBS** 15.2g | **SUGARS** 10g | **FIBER** 0.2g | **FAT** 41g

CHICKEN

YIELD: 4 servings | **PREP TIME:** 30 minutes (not including time to cook chicken) | **COOK TIME:** 35 minutes

This is a healthy makeover of a traditional pot pie recipe. You can also try the biscuit recipe on its own and pair it with other dishes, like Korean Sloppy Joes (page 115) or Cottage Cheese Egg Scramble (page 43). To do so, use a 3-tablespoon cookie scoop to form the dough into biscuits and bake on a parchment-lined baking sheet in a preheated 375°F oven for 20 minutes, or until golden brown.

BISCUITS:

- 1 cup rice flour
- 2 tablespoons potato flakes
- 1 teaspoon baking soda
- ¼ teaspoon Redmond Real Salt
- ⅔ cup full-fat buttermilk
- 2 teaspoons honey
- 2 tablespoons cold unsalted butter, finely diced
- 1 tablespoon unsalted butter, melted, for brushing

FILLING:

- 3 tablespoons unsalted butter
- 1 tablespoon extra-virgin olive oil
- 1 cup diced carrots
- 1 cup finely diced Yukon Gold potatoes
- ½ cup finely diced yellow onions
- 1 teaspoon Redmond Real Salt
- Leaves from 4 sprigs fresh thyme
- 2 cups chicken bone broth
- 1 cup whole milk
- 3 cloves garlic, minced
- 3 tablespoons arrowroot starch
- 4 cups shredded cooked chicken breast
- 1 cup frozen peas

1. Make the biscuit dough: Mix the rice flour, potato flakes, baking soda, and salt in a stand mixer fitted with the paddle attachment.
2. Add the buttermilk, honey, and 2 tablespoons of the butter. Mix on medium speed until just blended. Cover the bowl and refrigerate until ready to use.
3. Preheat the oven to 400°F.
4. Make the filling: Melt the butter in a large cast-iron skillet over medium heat. Pour in the olive oil. Add the carrots, potatoes, and onions. Cook, stirring occasionally, for 8 minutes, or until tender.
5. Season the vegetables with the salt and add the thyme.
6. Whisk together the broth, milk, garlic, and arrowroot in a medium bowl. Pour over the vegetables and continue to cook for about 5 minutes, allowing the mixture to thicken.
7. Stir in the chicken and peas. Remove the pan from the heat.
8. Using a 3-tablespoon cookie scoop, scoop eight biscuits out of the biscuit dough and arrange on top of the filling mixture. Brush the melted butter on each biscuit.
9. Put the skillet in the oven and bake for 18 minutes, or until the biscuits are golden brown. Let rest for 5 minutes before serving.

PER SERVING:
CALORIES 857 | **PROTEIN** 59.1g | **CARBS** 72.3g | **SUGARS** 13.3g | **FIBER** 6.18g | **FAT** 41g

GREEK TURKEY BURGERS
with Tzatziki

YIELD: 2 servings | **PREP TIME:** 10 minutes, plus 1 hour to chill tzatziki
COOK TIME: 14 minutes

These burgers are great for dinner or with a salad at lunch. Enjoy with romaine, escarole, or your favorite crunchy lettuce leaf.

TZATZIKI:

1 English cucumber, peeled and seeded

1 teaspoon Redmond Real Salt

1 cup plain Greek yogurt (5% fat)

1 tablespoon chopped fresh dill

2 cloves garlic, minced

1 teaspoon grated lemon zest

1 tablespoon lemon juice

⅛ teaspoon cracked black pepper

BURGERS:

12 ounces ground turkey (85% lean)

3 ounces feta cheese, crumbled

½ cup fresh spinach, finely chopped

¼ cup pitted Kalamata olives, finely chopped

1 teaspoon minced garlic

1 teaspoon dried oregano leaves (preferably Greek oregano)

½ teaspoon Redmond Real Salt

1 tablespoon avocado oil

1. Make the tzatziki: Grate the cucumber into a strainer set over a bowl. Sprinkle with the salt and allow to drain for 20 minutes. Squeeze the excess water out of the cucumber.
2. Mix together the cucumber, yogurt, dill, garlic, lemon zest and juice, and pepper. Cover and refrigerate for at least 1 hour.
3. Make the turkey burgers: Preheat the oven to 400°F.
4. Put the turkey, feta, spinach, olives, garlic, oregano, and salt in a medium bowl. Mix thoroughly. Form into four burgers about 1½ inches inch thick.
5. Heat the avocado oil in a large cast-iron skillet over medium-high heat. Pan-fry the burgers for about 3 minutes on each side, until browned.
6. Transfer the pan to the oven and cook for 8 minutes, or until the burgers are cooked through (the meat should no longer be pink in the center).
7. Let the burgers rest for 5 minutes. Serve with the tzatziki.

PER SERVING:
CALORIES 598 | **PROTEIN** 49.4g | **CARBS** 16.4g | **SUGARS** 6.3g | **FIBER** 2.2g | **FAT** 51.6g

BBQ TURKEY *Meatloaf*

YIELD: 4 servings | **PREP TIME:** 12 minutes (not including time to make sauce)
COOK TIME: 40 minutes

You can make this meatloaf with any of your favorite ground meats, whether chicken, bison, pork, or beef. Trying swapping out the traditional barbecue sauce for other sauces from the Dressing and Sauces section, like Japanese-Style BBQ Sauce (page 210) or Buffalo Sauce (page 212).

- 1 tablespoon avocado oil
- ½ cup finely diced carrots
- ½ cup finely diced celery
- ½ cup finely diced yellow onions
- ½ cup finely diced red bell peppers
- 1 pound ground turkey (85% lean)
- ½ cup quinoa flakes
- 1 large egg, beaten
- Leaves from 3 sprigs fresh thyme
- ¼ teaspoon grated lemon zest
- ¾ teaspoon Redmond Real Salt
- ½ cup BBQ Sauce (page 211)

1. Preheat the oven to 375°F. Line a sheet pan with parchment paper.
2. Heat the avocado oil in a large skillet over medium heat. Add the carrots, celery, onions, and bell peppers. Cook, stirring occasionally, for 5 minutes, or until tender. Remove the pan from the heat and allow to cool.
3. Using your hands, mix together the vegetables, turkey, quinoa flakes, egg, thyme, lemon zest, and salt in a medium bowl. Shape into 2 loaves and place on the prepared sheet pan.
4. Spoon the BBQ sauce over the loaves, coating them evenly.
5. Bake for 35 minutes, or until cooked to 165°F.
6. Slice the loaves into 4 pieces each, place 2 slices on each of 4 plates, and serve immediately.

PER SERVING:
CALORIES 293 | **PROTEIN** 30g | **CARBS** 17.6g | **SUGARS** 7.9g | **FIBER** 2.3g | **FAT** 9.5g

TURKEY Bean Chili

YIELD: 4 servings | **PREP TIME:** 15 minutes | **COOK TIME:** 40 minutes

This is a great dish to make ahead, portion out into individual servings, and store in the freezer. For added protein, top it with a dollop of plain Greek yogurt. Garnish with lime wedges and cilantro leaves.

1 tablespoon extra-virgin olive oil

1 pound ground turkey (85% lean)

½ teaspoon Redmond Real Salt

1 cup chopped yellow onions

2 cloves garlic, minced

1 cup chopped red bell peppers

½ cup chopped celery

1 jalapeño pepper, deveined, seeded, and finely chopped

1 teaspoon chopped fresh oregano leaves

1 bay leaf

1 tablespoon plus 1 teaspoon chili powder

1 teaspoon ground cumin

½ teaspoon ground coriander

2 cups canned diced tomatoes

1 cup chicken bone broth

1 (15-ounce) can red kidney beans, drained

1. Heat the olive oil in a 6-quart sauce pot over medium-high heat. Add the turkey and season with the salt. Cook, breaking up the turkey with a wooden spoon, until lightly browned, about 5 minutes.
2. Add the onions, garlic, bell peppers, celery, jalapeño, oregano, bay leaf, chili powder, cumin, and coriander. Cook for 5 minutes, stirring occasionally, or until tender.
3. Add the tomatoes and broth and bring to a boil. Lower the heat to a simmer and continue to cook, stirring occasionally, for 20 minutes.
4. Add the beans and cook for an additional 10 minutes, until thickened. Remove from the heat and serve.
5. Store in an airtight container in the refrigerator for up to 3 days.

PER SERVING:
CALORIES 352 | **PROTEIN** 35g | **CARBS** 33.2g | **SUGARS** 7.3g | **FIBER** 10.8g | **FAT** 8.8g

TURKEY

YIELD: 4 servings | **PREP TIME:** 10 minutes, plus 4 hours to marinate turkey (not including time to make rub) | **COOK TIME:** 45 minutes

If you have ever walked the streets of New York City, you undoubtedly know the aromas of the halal meat carts. This dish gives street meat a healthy makeover. Serve with a simple chopped salad of tomatoes, cucumbers, and red onions and drizzle with Green Tahini Dressing (page 214).

1 cup plain Greek yogurt (5% fat)

Juice of ½ lemon

3 tablespoon Shawarma Salt Rub (page 224)

1 small boneless, skinless turkey breast (about 1 pound)

1. In a medium bowl, mix together the yogurt, lemon juice, and salt rub.
2. Rub the turkey with the yogurt marinade, coating it evenly. Transfer to an airtight container and refrigerate for 4 hours or, for maximum flavor, overnight.
3. Preheat the oven to 350°F. Line a sheet pan with parchment paper.
4. Remove the turkey breast from the marinade and shake off any excess. Place the turkey on the prepared sheet pan.
5. Bake the turkey for 45 minutes, or until the internal temperature hits 165°F. Let rest for 10 minutes before slicing and serving.
6. Store in an airtight container in the refrigerator for up to 3 days.

PER SERVING:
CALORIES 169 | **PROTEIN** 31g | **CARBS** 2.5g | **SUGARS** 1.9g | **FIBER** 0g | **FAT** 4g

BEEF, BISON, *and* LAMB

BEEF BOLOGNESE *with Spaghetti Squash*

YIELD: 4 servings | **PREP TIME:** 15 minutes | **COOK TIME:** 50 minutes

This is a great make-ahead recipe to freeze for meal prep. Here the sauce is served over spaghetti squash, but feel free to play around with different veggie noodles and pastas, like butternut squash noodles or chickpea or brown rice pasta.

3 tablespoons extra-virgin olive oil, divided

¾ cup finely diced yellow onions

1 carrot, cut into small dice

2 stalks celery, cut into small dice

2 cloves garlic, smashed with the side of a knife

1 pound ground beef

2 teaspoons Redmond Real Salt, divided

1 cup dry red wine

1 cup beef bone broth

¾ cup tomato paste

4 sprigs fresh thyme

1 bay leaf

1 small spaghetti squash (about 3 pounds)

2 tablespoons grated Parmesan cheese, for serving

1. Heat 1 tablespoon of the olive oil in a 6-quart stockpot over medium heat. Add the onions, carrot, and celery and cook, stirring occasionally, for 5 minutes, or until the onions are translucent. Add the garlic and cook for an additional minute.
2. Add the beef and season with 1½ teaspoons of the salt. Cook, stirring continuously to break up the clumps, until the meat is nicely browned, about 6 minutes.
3. Add the wine, broth, tomato paste, thyme sprigs, and bay leaf to the pot. Reduce the heat to low and simmer uncovered for 40 minutes. While the Bolognese is simmering, prepare the squash.
4. Preheat the oven to 400°F and line a sheet pan with parchment paper.
5. Cut the spaghetti squash in half lengthwise. Using a large spoon, scrape out the seeds. Brush the inside of the squash with the remaining 2 tablespoons of olive oil and season with the remaining ½ teaspoon of salt. Place flesh side down on the prepared pan.
6. Bake the squash for 30 minutes, or until tender. Allow to cool slightly, then use a large spoon to scrape the strands of squash from inside the skin.
7. To serve, remove the thyme stems and bay leaf from the Bolognese, then spoon the sauce over the spaghetti squash and sprinkle with the Parmesan.
8. The Bolognese sauce may be made ahead and stored in an airtight container in the refrigerator for up to 3 days or in the freezer for up to 3 months. The squash may be made ahead and stored in a separate container in the refrigerator for up to 3 days.

PER SERVING:
CALORIES 521 | **PROTEIN** 28.2g | **CARBS** 27.1g | **SUGARS** 13.9g | **FIBER** 5.4g | **FAT** 28.1g

GINGER LEMONGRASS *Flanken Ribs*

YIELD: 2 servings | **PREP TIME:** 12 minutes, plus 1 hour to marinate | **COOK TIME:** 6 minutes

Don't want to wait hours for bone-in beef ribs to cook? Try these thin-cut flanken ribs for a quick weeknight dish. When shopping, you might find them called thin-cut bone-in short ribs, flanken-style. Serve them with Broccoli Stem Slaw (page 163) or your favorite veggie side.

MARINADE:

2 cloves garlic, roughly chopped

2 teaspoons grated fresh ginger

1 stalk lemongrass, outer stem removed, roughly chopped

1 serrano pepper, roughly chopped

1 tablespoon honey

1 tablespoon extra-virgin olive oil

1 tablespoon untoasted sesame oil

1 tablespoon tamari

2 pounds bone-in flanken ribs

½ teaspoon Redmond Real Salt

FOR GARNISH:

1 teaspoon white sesame seeds

2 scallions, sliced

1 tablespoon fresh cilantro leaves

1 lime, cut into wedges

1. Make the marinade: Blend the garlic, ginger, lemongrass, serrano pepper, honey, olive oil, sesame oil, and tamari in a blender.
2. Season the ribs with the salt, then coat with the marinade. Place in an airtight container and refrigerate for at least 1 hour or overnight.
3. Preheat a grill or large grill pan on the stovetop to medium heat.
4. Scrape off the excess marinade. Grill the ribs for about 3 minutes on each side, until browned. Remove from the heat and let rest for 5 minutes.
5. To serve, garnish with the sesame seeds, scallions, cilantro, and lime wedges.

PER SERVING:

CALORIES 538 | **PROTEIN** 42g | **CARBS** 5.4g | **SUGARS** 4.4g | **FIBER** 0.2g | **FAT** 116.3g

BEEF & BROCCOLI

YIELD: 2 servings | **PREP TIME:** 12 minutes | **COOK TIME:** 8 minutes

This classic stir-fry won't disappoint. Try serving it with rice or your favorite rice noodle. You can play around with other proteins, like chicken.

2 cups broccoli florets

1 tablespoon Redmond Real Salt

⅓ cup beef bone broth

¼ cup tamari

1½ tablespoons honey

1 teaspoon grated fresh ginger

1½ tablespoons arrowroot starch

1 tablespoon avocado oil

1 pound boneless grass-fed sirloin steak, thinly sliced

2 cloves garlic, thinly sliced

1 teaspoon white sesame seeds, for garnish

1. Fill a medium bowl with ice water.
2. Bring a medium pot of water to a rolling boil. Add the broccoli and salt and cook for 3 minutes, or until crisp-tender. Drain the water and submerge the broccoli in the ice bath for 3 minutes to stop the cooking. Remove from the ice bath and pat dry. Set aside.
3. Whisk together the broth, tamari, honey, ginger, and arrowroot in a small bowl until the arrowroot has dissolved. Set aside.
4. Heat the avocado oil in a wok or large skillet over high heat. Add the steak and garlic and sear for 1 minute on each side. Add the broth mixture and broccoli and cook until the broth has thickened, about 2 minutes.
5. To serve, garnish the beef and broccoli with the sesame seeds.

PER SERVING:
CALORIES 700 | **PROTEIN** 51.6g | **CARBS** 25.1g | **SUGARS** 14.5g | **FIBER** 2.8g | **FAT** 43.2g

STEAK

YIELD: 2 servings | **PREP TIME:** 10 minutes (not including time to make dressing)
COOK TIME: 10 minutes

This salad is full of hydrating ingredients and crunchy textures. You can top it with any protein, such as salmon, shrimp, or chicken.

- 1 tablespoon avocado oil
- 1 (12-ounce) boneless New York strip steak, about 1½ inches thick
- ¾ teaspoon Redmond Real Salt
- ½ cup bean sprouts
- 2 Persian or other small seedless cucumbers, thinly sliced
- 1 large carrot, julienned
- 1 small watermelon radish, thinly sliced
- 3 scallions, chopped
- 1 serrano pepper, seeded and thinly sliced
- 1 tablespoon fresh cilantro leaves
- 2 tablespoons Banh Mi Dressing (page 216)
- 2 heads gem lettuce, cut into quarters
- 2 teaspoons finely chopped fresh chives, for garnish

1. Heat the avocado oil in a medium cast-iron skillet over medium-high heat.
2. Pat the steak dry with a paper towel and season with the salt. For medium-rare meat, sear the steak in the hot oil for 5 minutes on each side, or until the internal temperature is 130°F. (If you prefer more or less done meat, adjust the cooking time accordingly.) Remove from the pan and allow to rest for at least 5 minutes. Cut into thin slices and set aside.
3. Combine the bean sprouts, cucumbers, carrot, radish, scallions, serrano pepper, and cilantro in a medium bowl. Add the dressing and toss, making sure the vegetable mixture is evenly coated.
4. To serve, top the quartered lettuce with the bean sprout mixture and the sliced steak. Garnish with the chives.

PER SERVING:
CALORIES 521 | **PROTEIN** 43.4g | **CARBS** 17.9g | **SUGARS** 9.4g | **FIBER** 8.2g | **FAT** 28.9g

BACON JAM BURGER
Collard Wraps

YIELD: 2 burgers | **PREP TIME:** 15 minutes (not including time to make jam)
COOK TIME: 9 minutes

Collard wraps are an amazing alternative to a traditional bun. Ditching the bun allows you to add more nutrient-dense calories to your burger, like eggs and bacon.

2 tablespoons plus 1¾ teaspoons Redmond Real Salt, divided

4 collard greens, thick ribs and stems removed

12 ounces ground beef (85% lean)

2 tablespoons avocado oil, divided

2 large eggs

3 tablespoons Bacon Jam (page 221)

1. Fill a large bowl with ice water.
2. Bring a large pot of water to a boil. Add 2 tablespoons of the salt. Cook the collard greens in the boiling water for 45 seconds. Drain the water and submerge the collards in the ice water until fully cooled, about 2 minutes. Remove from the water and pat dry with a paper towel. Set aside.
3. Form the beef into two 4-inch-wide patties. Season the tops and bottoms with 1½ teaspoons of the salt.
4. Heat 1 tablespoon of the avocado oil in a large skillet over medium-high heat. Once hot, add the burgers and cook to desired doneness, 3 to 4 minutes per side for medium. Remove from the pan and allow to rest for 8 minutes.
5. While the burgers are resting, heat the remaining tablespoon of avocado oil in a nonstick skillet over medium-low heat. Gently crack the eggs into the pan and season with the remaining ¼ teaspoon of salt. Cover with a lid and cook for 2 minutes, or until the whites are cooked and the yolks are cooked medium. Remove the pan from the heat.
6. To construct the wraps, top the burgers with an even layer of the bacon jam. Top each with an egg. Place 2 collard greens on a cutting board with the stem ends overlapping. Lay a burger on one short end and roll up, tucking the collards around the burger until it's completely enclosed. Repeat with the remaining collards and burger.
7. To serve, cut the wraps in half with a sharp knife.

PER SERVING:
CALORIES 625 | **PROTEIN** 48.8g | **CARBS** 15.5g | **SUGARS** 6g | **FIBER** 3g | **FAT** 43.8g

TUSCAN KALE CAESAR *with Smoky Filet Mignon & Sweet Potato Croutons*

YIELD: 2 servings | **PREP TIME:** 20 minutes, plus 1 hour to marinate beef (not including time to make salt rub or dressing) | **COOK TIME:** 30 minutes

You can swap out any of your favorite hearty lettuces for the kale in this salad. Try romaine, escarole, or gem lettuce for a great crunch.

2 (5-ounce) filets mignons, about 1½ inches thick

2 tablespoons Smoky Steak Salt Rub (page 224)

1 tablespoon avocado oil, for the pan

CROUTONS:

1 large sweet potato (about 14 ounces), peeled and cut into ½-inch dice

1 tablespoon extra-virgin olive oil

1 tablespoon grated Pecorino Romano cheese

2 teaspoons tapioca starch

2 teaspoons dried parsley

½ teaspoon garlic powder

½ teaspoon Redmond Real Salt

SALAD:

1 bunch Tuscan kale, stems and thick ribs removed

¼ small red onion, thinly sliced

2 tablespoons High-Protein Caesar Dressing (page 217)

1. Season all sides of the filets with the salt rub. Cover and refrigerate for at least 1 hour or overnight.
2. Remove the filets from the refrigerator and allow them to sit out on the counter for 30 minutes. While the filets are tempering, make the croutons.
3. Preheat the oven or an air fryer to 400°F. Line a sheet pan or the air fryer tray with parchment paper.
4. In a medium bowl, toss the sweet potato in the olive oil, cheese, tapioca starch, parsley, garlic powder, and salt. Spread on the prepared pan or tray and bake or air-fry for 22 minutes, or until golden brown and cooked through. Remove from the oven and set aside.
5. Cook the filets: Heat the avocado oil in a medium skillet over medium-high heat. Once the oil is hot, add the filets and sear on both sides, about 4 minutes on each side, until cooked to medium-rare. Remove the steaks from the pan and transfer to a cutting board to rest for 8 minutes before slicing.
6. Make the salad: Put the kale and onions in a large bowl and toss with the Caesar dressing.
7. To serve, plate the salad and sprinkle the sweet potato croutons on top. Arrange the sliced beef on top.

PER SERVING:
CALORIES 660 | **PROTEIN** 35.1g | **CARBS** 27g | **SUGARS** 5.4g | **FIBER** 4.6g | **FAT** 47g

BISON OSSO BUCO *with Walnut Gremolata*

YIELD: 4 servings | **PREP TIME:** 18 minutes | **COOK TIME:** 2 hours 45 minutes

Osso buco is traditionally made with veal shanks, but here we use bison shanks. This recipe can also be made with grass-fed beef. This is a great make-ahead dish that tastes even better when reheated the next day. Serve it with High-Protein Mashed Potatoes (page 155).

GREMOLATA:

2 tablespoons raw walnuts

¼ cup fresh parsley leaves

1 teaspoon grated lemon zest

1 tablespoon extra-virgin olive oil

OSSO BUCO:

3 pounds bison shanks, each about 2 inches thick (aka bison osso buco)

1½ teaspoons Redmond Real Salt

2 tablespoons avocado oil

1 large yellow onion, cut into ½-inch dice

2 carrots, cut into ½-inch dice

2 stalks celery, cut into ½-inch dice

½ cup red wine

4 cloves garlic, smashed with the side of a knife

3 sprigs fresh thyme

1 bay leaf

1½ cups beef bone broth

28 ounces diced tomatoes

1. Make the gremolata: Toast the walnuts in a small skillet over low heat for 3 minutes. Remove from the pan and let cool completely, then finely chop the nuts.
2. Mix the toasted walnuts, parsley, lemon zest, and olive oil in a small bowl. Cover and store in the refrigerator until ready to serve (can be made 1 day in advance).
3. Prepare the osso buco: Preheat the oven to 350°F.
4. Pat the bison shanks dry with a paper towel. Season with the salt.
5. Heat the avocado oil in a Dutch oven over high heat. Once the oil is hot, work in batches to brown the shanks on both sides, about 3 minutes per side. Remove from the pot and set aside.
6. Lower the heat to medium. Add the onion, carrots, and celery to the pot. Cook for 4 minutes, or until the vegetables are tender. Add the wine and deglaze the pot with a wooden spoon, scraping up any caramelized bits of meat stuck to the bottom. Add the garlic, thyme, bay leaf, broth, and tomatoes and bring to a boil.
7. Return the shanks to the pot. Cover with the lid and place in the oven. Cook for 2½ hours, or until the meat is falling off the bone. Baste the shanks every 30 minutes and turn them over halfway through cooking.
8. Remove the pot from the oven. Skim off any excess fat. Discard the bay leaf and thyme stems.
9. To serve, remove the shanks from the pot with a slotted spoon. Spoon the gravy over the shanks and top with the gremolata.

PER SERVING:
CALORIES 550 | **PROTEIN** 37.5g | **CARBS** 20g | **SUGARS** 7.5g | **FIBER** 5g | **FAT** 35g

BISON MEATBALLS *in Tomato Sauce*

YIELD: 4 servings | **PREP TIME:** 10 minutes | **COOK TIME:** 25 minutes

These bison meatballs are great over spaghetti squash or your favorite pasta alternative. This recipe works well with ground elk, too.

TOMATO SAUCE:

1 tablespoon extra-virgin olive oil

¼ cup thinly sliced yellow onions

2 cloves garlic, minced

1 sprig fresh oregano

1 (14-ounce) can whole peeled San Marzano tomatoes, chopped

MEATBALLS:

1 tablespoon extra-virgin olive oil

½ cup finely diced yellow onions

1 pound ground bison

¼ cup quinoa flakes

2 tablespoons grated Parmesan cheese

1½ teaspoons Redmond Real Salt

1 large egg

2 teaspoons chopped fresh Italian parsley

½ teaspoon fresh thyme leaves

5 fresh basil leaves, torn, for garnish

1. Heat the olive oil in a large skillet over medium heat. Add the sliced onions and sauté until translucent, about 5 minutes. Add the garlic and oregano and continue cooking for 1 minute, until aromatic. Stir in the tomatoes with their liquid, lower the heat to a simmer, and continue to cook for 20 minutes. While the tomato mixture is simmering, prepare the meatballs.
2. Preheat the oven to 400°F. Line a sheet pan with parchment paper.
3. Heat the olive oil in a small skillet over medium heat. Add the diced onions and sauté until translucent, about 5 minutes. Remove the pan from the heat and allow to cool.
4. Put the cooled onions and the rest of the meatball ingredients in a medium bowl. Using your hands, mix until thoroughly combined.
5. Using a 2-tablespoon cookie scoop, form the meat mixture into 1-inch balls and arrange on the prepared pan. Spread out evenly. Bake for 10 minutes, or until browned.
6. Spoon the meatballs into the tomato mixture and simmer for 5 minutes to finish cooking them.
7. To serve, garnish with the torn basil leaves.
8. Store the meatballs and sauce in an airtight container in the refrigerator for up to 3 days or in the freezer for up to 3 months.

PER SERVING:
CALORIES 317 | **PROTEIN** 27.8g | **CARBS** 12g | **SUGARS** 3.8g | **FIBER** 2.6g | **FAT** 18.5g

THYME ROASTED MARROW BONES *with Bacon Jam*

YIELD: 4 servings | **PREP TIME:** 5 minutes (not including time to make jam)
COOK TIME: 10 minutes

Collagen is pure scoopable deliciousness straight from the source. When ordering marrow bones from your butcher, be sure that they are from cows that were 100 percent grass-fed. Ask the butcher to split the bones lengthwise for a great presentation and to make it easier to scoop out the marrow.

4 large beef marrow bones (about 3½ pounds), split lengthwise

¼ teaspoon Redmond Real Salt

¼ teaspoon cracked black pepper

1 clove garlic, minced

½ teaspoon grated lemon zest

4 sprigs fresh thyme

FOR SERVING:

3 tablespoons Bacon Jam (page 221)

1 tablespoon fresh parsley leaves

1. Preheat the oven to 375°F. Line a sheet pan with parchment paper.
2. Put the marrow bones cut side up on the prepared pan. Season with the salt and pepper, then sprinkle with the garlic and lemon zest. Top with the thyme sprigs.
3. Roast for 10 minutes, or until the marrow has started pulling away from the bone.
4. To serve, top with the bacon jam and parsley.

PER SERVING:
CALORIES 450 | **PROTEIN** 12.5g | **CARBS** 2.5g | **SUGARS** 2.5g | **FIBER** .5g | **FAT** 40g

GRILLED LAMB LOIN CHOPS *with Pomegranate, Mint & Green Tahini Dressing*

YIELD: 2 servings | **PREP TIME:** 5 minutes, plus 1 hour to marinate meat (not including time to make dressing) | **COOK TIME:** 9 minutes

You can serve this dish with High-Protein Mashed Potatoes (page 155). Or, if you want a real showstopper of a plate, try making green tahini potatoes by mixing ¼ cup of Green Tahini Dressing into 2 cups of the mashed potatoes.

1½ pounds grass-fed lamb loin chops, about 2 inches thick

1 tablespoon avocado oil

2 cloves garlic, smashed with the side of a knife

2 sprigs fresh rosemary

2 sprigs fresh thyme

½ teaspoon Redmond Real Salt

¼ teaspoon cracked black pepper

FOR SERVING:

¼ cup Green Tahini Dressing (page 214)

½ cup pomegranate arils

1 tablespoon fresh mint leaves

1. Pat the chops dry with a paper towel. Rub the lamb chops with the avocado oil. Then rub the garlic into the lamb and top with the rosemary and thyme sprigs. Cover and refrigerate for at least 1 hour or overnight.
2. Remove the chops from the refrigerator and allow to sit out on the counter for 30 minutes. Season with the salt and pepper.
3. Preheat a grill or grill pan on the stovetop to high heat.
4. Grill the chops on each side for 3 minutes. Remove from the heat and allow to rest for at least 5 minutes.
5. To serve, evenly spoon the dressing onto a platter, then top with the chops, pomegranate arils, and mint.

PER SERVING:
CALORIES 600 | **PROTEIN** 50g | **CARBS** 12.9g | **SUGARS** 6g | **FIBER** 3g | **FAT** 35g

ZA'ATAR-CRUSTED LAMB TENDERLOIN *with Shaved Fennel & Whipped Feta*

YIELD: 2 servings | **PREP TIME:** 15 minutes | **COOK TIME:** 6 minutes

Serve this dish on its own or with Crispy Smashed Yukon Golds (page 157). The potatoes are great dipped in the whipped feta.

WHIPPED FETA:

4 ounces feta cheese, crumbled

1 tablespoons extra-virgin olive oil

¼ cup whole milk

½ teaspoon grated lemon zest

1 tablespoon lemon juice

FENNEL SALAD:

1 small fennel bulb

1 teaspoon chopped fennel fronds

¼ teaspoon grated lemon zest

Juice of 1 lemon

1 tablespoon extra-virgin olive oil

¼ teaspoon Redmond Real Salt

LAMB:

1 pound lamb tenderloins

½ teaspoon Redmond Real Salt

2 tablespoons za'atar spice

1 tablespoon avocado oil

1. Make the whipped feta: Put the feta, olive oil, milk, and lemon zest and juice in a food processor. Blend until smooth and creamy. Transfer to an airtight container and refrigerate until ready to serve. May be prepared up to 1 day in advance.
2. Prepare a medium bowl of ice water. Thinly slice the fennel on a mandoline. (If you don't have a mandoline, use a sharp chef's knife.) Submerge the fennel in the ice water for about 10 minutes. Drain the fennel and pat dry. Toss in a medium bowl with the fennel fronds, lemon zest and juice, olive oil, and salt. Cover and refrigerate until serving. Can be made up to 4 hours ahead.
3. Pat the lamb dry with a paper towel. Season with the salt. Rub with the za'atar, being sure to coat the lamb evenly.
4. Heat the avocado oil in a large cast-iron skillet over medium-high heat. Sear the lamb for a total of 6 minutes, turning it every couple of minutes to brown it on all sides. Be careful not to burn the spice rub; lower the heat to medium, if needed. The lamb will be medium-rare.
5. Remove the pan from the heat and let the lamb rest on the cutting board for at least 5 minutes before cutting into ½-inch slices.
6. To serve, spoon the whipped feta onto two plates, then top the feta with the fennel salad. Fan the meat next to it.

PER SERVING:
CALORIES 780 | **PROTEIN** 40g | **CARBS** 7g | **SUGARS** 3g | **FIBER** 2g | **FAT** 65g

PORK

PORK

YIELD: 4 servings | **PREP TIME:** 15 minutes | **COOK TIME:** 12 minutes

This dish is a great base for Chicory Salad with Figs (page 177). But really, it can be mixed and matched with any of the veggie sides in this book.

4 (4-ounce) boneless pork loin chops, pounded to ¼ inch thick

¼ teaspoon Redmond Real Salt

1 cup quinoa flakes

½ cup grated Parmesan cheese

1 teaspoon dried parsley

½ cup arrowroot starch

2 large eggs

4 tablespoons extra-virgin olive oil, divided

1. Preheat the oven to 200°F. Line a sheet pan with parchment paper.
2. Season the pork chops on both sides with the salt. Set aside.
3. Mix together the quinoa, Parmesan cheese, and parsley in a medium shallow bowl.
4. Create a dredging station by placing the arrowroot and eggs in separate shallow bowls. Beat the eggs. Have the bowl with the quinoa mixture nearby.
5. Dip a pork chop into the arrowroot, shaking off any excess, then dredge it in the eggs and then in the quinoa mixture. Be sure to coat the chop evenly on both sides. Repeat with the second chop.
6. Heat 2 tablespoons of the olive oil in a large skillet over medium heat. When the oil is hot, place a pork chop in the pan and cook for 3 minutes on each side, or until golden brown. Transfer to the lined sheet pan and hold in the oven to keep warm.
7. Wipe the skillet clean with a paper towel. Return the pan to the heat, pour in the remaining 2 tablespoons of olive oil, and cook the second pork chop as directed in Step 6.
8. Serve immediately.

PER SERVING:
CALORIES 491 | **PROTEIN** 30.3g | **CARBS** 25.1g | **SUGARS** 0.25g | **FIBER** 1.8g | **FAT** 30g

KOREAN SLOPPY JOES
with Quick Pickles

YIELD: 2 servings | **PREP TIME:** 8 minutes, plus 1 hour to pickle cucumbers and marinate meat | **COOK TIME:** 10 minutes

This dish is layered with flavors. Enjoy it straight up, with a spoon, or use it as filling for lettuce wraps to enjoy as a sandwich, like the sloppy joes of childhood but better. Make a double batch and save the leftovers for the next day.

PICKLES:

2 Persian or other small seedless cucumbers, thinly sliced

¼ cup rice wine vinegar

1 teaspoon Redmond Real Salt

½ teaspoon black sesame seeds, for garnish

SLOPPY JOE MIXTURE:

1 pound ground pork

4 cloves garlic, minced

1 (1-inch) knob ginger, grated

¼ cup gochujang sauce

1 teaspoon untoasted sesame oil

1 teaspoon tamari

1 tablespoon extra-virgin olive oil

¾ cup diced yellow onions

FOR GARNISH/SERVING:

1 scallion, sliced

1 tablespoon fresh cilantro leaves (optional)

Lettuce leaves

1. Make the pickles: Combine the cucumbers, vinegar, and salt in a small bowl. Cover and refrigerate for at least 1 hour.
2. Put the ground pork, garlic, ginger, gochujang, sesame oil, and tamari in a medium bowl. Using your hands, mix until well combined. Cover and refrigerate for at least 1 hour.
3. Heat a large skillet over medium heat. Pour in the olive oil, add the onions, and sauté until translucent, about 5 minutes.
4. Add the pork mixture and cook, stirring continuously to break up the clumps, for about 5 minutes, until browned. Remove from the heat and drain off any excess fat.
5. To serve, garnish the meat with the scallion and cilantro, if using. Garnish the pickles with the sesame seeds and serve alongside the pork mixture. If desired, use the pork mixture and pickles to fill lettuce wraps and enjoy as a sandwich.

PER SERVING:
CALORIES 708 | **PROTEIN** 28.9g | **CARBS** 22.5g | **SUGARS** 10.7g | **FIBER** 3.5g | **FAT** 54.2g

ZUCCHINI NOODLE *Lasagna*

YIELD: 4 servings | **PREP TIME:** 25 minutes | **COOK TIME:** 50 minutes

Zucchini cut into planks is a great alternative to pasta noodles in lasagna. You can pair them with any meat filling you prefer. (Here we use equal parts pork and beef.) The only trick is to cook the zucchini before layering it into the lasagna to remove the excess water.

2 pounds zucchini

3 tablespoons extra-virgin olive oil, divided

1½ teaspoons Redmond Real Salt, divided

¾ cup diced yellow onions

8 ounces ground beef

8 ounces ground pork

2 cloves garlic, minced

3 fresh sage leaves

8 ounces baby spinach

1 cup no-sugar-added tomato sauce

8 ounces fresh mozzarella cheese, cut into small dice

¾ cup ricotta cheese

¼ cup shredded mozzarella cheese

1. Preheat the oven to 300°F. Line two sheet pans with parchment paper.
2. Trim the zucchini ends. Using a mandoline, slice the zucchini lengthwise into planks about ⅛ inch thick. (If you don't have a mandoline, use a sharp chef's knife.) Spread out the zucchini on the prepared pans. Brush with 2 tablespoons of the olive oil and season with ¾ teaspoon of the salt. Bake for 20 minutes, or until tender but not browned. While the zucchini is in the oven, prepare the meat filling.
3. Heat a large skillet over medium heat. Pour in the remaining tablespoon of olive oil, add the onions, and sauté until translucent, about 5 minutes. Add the beef, pork, garlic, sage, and remaining ¾ teaspoon of salt. Cook, stirring continuously, until the meat is completely cooked with no pink remaining, about 6 minutes. Remove from the heat. Drain the excess fat and set the pan aside.
4. When the zucchini is done, remove it from the oven and allow to cool until it's safe to handle. Once cool, remove from the pan and pat dry with paper towels.
5. Increase the oven temperature to 350°F.
6. Assemble the lasagna: Coat the bottom of a 9 by 13-inch baking dish with 1 tablespoon of the tomato sauce. Line with slices of zucchini to make the first layer. Spread 1 tablespoon of sauce on the zucchini. Add a layer of meat and top with few leaves of spinach. Add a sprinkle of diced mozzarella and ricotta. Repeat the layers, reserving 1 tablespoon of sauce for the top and ending with a layer of zucchini. Top the lasagna with the reserved tomato sauce and sprinkle the shredded mozzarella evenly on the top.

7. Bake for 30 minutes, or until the cheese is slightly golden and bubbly. Serve immediately.
8. Store covered in the refrigerator for up to 3 days or in the freezer for up to 3 months.

PER SERVING:
CALORIES 747 | **PROTEIN** 46.7g | **CARBS** 19.6g | **SUGARS** 8.8g | **FIBER** 4.9g | **FAT** 55.3g

CHILE LIME SALT-RUBBED
Pork Flank Steak

YIELD: 2 servings | **PREP TIME:** 4 minutes, plus 30 minutes to marinate steak (not including time to make salt rub) | **COOK TIME:** 14 minutes

As with any recipe using pork, using a heritage breed of pork, humanely raised, reaps flavor and nutrition dividends. One of our favorite breeds for pork is the Iberico pig from Spain. It is like no other. The pigs feed on acorns, giving the meat a rich, nutty taste and a higher fat content. For a stronger spice flavor, use more Chile Lime Salt Rub.

1 pound pork flank steak (aka boneless pork butt steak)

2 tablespoons Chile Lime Salt Rub (page 223), or more to taste

1. Trim any excess fat from the pork flank. Place the flank on a parchment-lined sheet pan.
2. Coat both sides of the flank steak evenly with the salt rub, packing it into the meat. Allow to rest and absorb the flavors for 30 minutes.
3. Preheat the oven to 375°F.
4. Bake the flank steak for 14 minutes, or until the meat reaches 145°F and the rub is caramelized. Remove from the oven and allow to rest for 10 minutes before slicing and serving.

PER SERVING:
CALORIES 689 | **PROTEIN** 49.4g | **CARBS** 2.2g | **SUGARS** 0g | **FIBER** 1.1g | **FAT** 54.5g

BBQ

YIELD: 6 servings | **PREP TIME:** 20 minutes, plus 1 hour to marinate pork (not including time to make sauce) | **COOK TIME:** 3 hours

This is a great large-batch recipe to make ahead and freeze individual portions for weeknight dinners. Serve with your favorite slaw.

1 tablespoon paprika

2½ teaspoons Redmond Real Salt

½ teaspoon ground cumin

½ teaspoon garlic powder

¼ teaspoon mustard powder

2½ pounds boneless pork shoulder

1 cup water

¾ cup BBQ Sauce (page 211), warmed

1. Whisk together the paprika, salt, cumin, garlic powder, and mustard powder in a small bowl.
2. Coat the pork shoulder evenly with the spice mixture. Cover and refrigerate for at least 1 hour or overnight.
3. Preheat the oven to 300°F.
4. Put the pork shoulder in a roasting pan. Pour the water into the pan.
5. Cover and bake for 2½ to 3 hours, until the meat is so tender that you can easily shred it with two forks. Remove from the oven and allow to cool, then shred the pork.
6. Toss the shredded pork in a large bowl with the BBQ sauce until evenly coated. Serve immediately.
7. Store in an airtight container in the refrigerator for up to 4 days or in the freezer for up to 3 months.

PER SERVING:

CALORIES 710 | **PROTEIN** 55.9g | **CARBS** 7g | **SUGARS** 5.3g | **FIBER** 0.5g | **FAT** 50.9g

VENISON

PROSCIUTTO-WRAPPED *Venison Tenderloin*

YIELD: 2 servings | **PREP TIME:** 8 minutes | **COOK TIME:** 12 minutes

With venison, you always want to cook the meat no further than medium-rare to create the perfect texture. Serve this dish with Brussels Sprout Slaw (page 165).

2 (5-ounce) venison tenderloins

1 teaspoon Redmond Real Salt

3 cloves garlic, minced

6 pieces prosciutto, thinly sliced

6 fresh basil leaves

1½ tablespoons avocado oil

1. Preheat the oven to 400°F.
2. Pat the tenderloins dry with a paper towel. Season with the salt. Rub evenly with the minced garlic.
3. To assemble, place a piece of parchment paper on a cutting board. Lay 3 slices of prosciutto lengthwise, overlapping by ⅓ inch. Spread 3 basil leaves on top of the prosciutto. Place a tenderloin close to the edge of the prosciutto slices and then tightly roll it up, making sure the tenderloin is completely encased in the prosciutto. Repeat with the remaining tenderloin, prosciutto, and basil.
4. Heat the avocado oil in a large cast-iron skillet or other heavy ovenproof pan over medium-high heat. When the oil is hot, sear the tenderloins for 2 minutes on each side. You want the prosciutto to start to crisp and lightly brown.
5. Transfer the pan to the oven and bake until the internal temperature of the tenderloins is between 125°F and 130°F, about 7 minutes.
6. Remove the tenderloins to a cutting board and allow to rest for at least 5 minutes before slicing. Cut each tenderloin into 3 slices and enjoy.

PER SERVING:
CALORIES 382 | **PROTEIN** 44.4g | **CARBS** 1.7g | **SUGARS** 0g | **FIBER** 0.2g | **FAT** 19.5g

JERK VENISON RIB CHOPS
with Jicama Mango Salsa

YIELD: 2 servings | **PREP TIME:** 15 minutes, plus 1 hour to marinate chops
COOK TIME: 8 minutes

Serve this dish with High-Protein Mashed Potatoes (page 155). The yogurt in the mashed potatoes has a cooling effect that works well with the jerk spice on the ribs. For a hotter jerk, leave the seeds and ribs in the jalapeño. Want to take the heat up another notch? Swap out the jalapeño for a habanero.

JICAMA MANGO SALSA:

½ small jicama, peeled and cut into ¼-inch dice

1 mango, peeled and cut into ¼-inch dice

½ shallot, finely chopped

1 serrano chile, ribbed, seeded, and finely chopped

1 tablespoon extra-virgin olive oil

Juice of 1 lime

¼ teaspoon Redmond Real Salt

JERK PASTE:

2 tablespoons avocado oil or beef tallow

Juice of 1 lime

1 (1-inch) knob fresh ginger, grated

2 cloves garlic, minced

¼ cup coconut sugar

1 teaspoon tamari

1 jalapeño pepper, deveined, seeded, and finely chopped

1 teaspoon fresh thyme leaves

6 fresh basil leaves, torn

1 teaspoon chili powder

½ teaspoon ground coriander

¼ teaspoon ground allspice

¼ teaspoon ground cinnamon

¼ teaspoon ground nutmeg

¼ teaspoon cracked black pepper

1 teaspoon Redmond Real Salt

1½ pounds bone-in venison rib chops, about 1½ inches thick

2 sprigs fresh mint, for garnish

1. Combine all of the ingredients for the salsa in a medium bowl. Cover and refrigerate. (The salsa can be made 2 hours ahead.)
2. In a small bowl, mix together the ingredients for the jerk paste.
3. Pat the rib chops dry with a paper towel. Coat both sides of the chops with the jerk paste. Cover and refrigerate for at least 1 hour or overnight for bigger flavor.
4. Remove the rib chops from the refrigerator and allow them to sit out on the counter for 20 minutes.
5. Heat a grill or large grill pan on the stovetop to medium-high heat. Grill the chops for 3 to 4 minutes on each side, until cooked to medium-rare.
6. Allow the chops to rest for 5 minutes before serving. To serve, top with the salsa and garnish with a sprig of mint.

PER SERVING:
CALORIES 792 | **PROTEIN** 89g | **CARBS** 48.4g | **SUGARS** 36.3g | **FIBER** 4.9g | **FAT** 33.6g

CAST-IRON ELK STEAK with Rosemary Garlic Butter

YIELD: 2 servings | **PREP TIME:** 1 minute | **COOK TIME:** 7 minutes

Elk, like venison, is best cooked to medium-rare at most to maintain the meat's flavor and tenderness. Serve this dish with Crispy Smashed Yukon Golds (page 157) and your favorite greens.

- 2 (6-ounce) boneless elk New York strip steaks, about 1½ inches thick
- 1 teaspoon Redmond Real Salt
- 2 tablespoons unsalted butter
- 3 sprigs fresh rosemary
- 2 cloves garlic, smashed with the side of a knife

1. Season the steaks with the salt.
2. Heat a large cast-iron skillet over high heat. When the pan is hot, add the butter and both steaks, making sure there is plenty of room between them. Put the rosemary sprigs and garlic cloves in the pan. Tilt the pan slightly by the handle so the butter pools at the edge. Using a tablespoon, continuously baste the steaks with garlic butter mixture. Don't allow the garlic to brown; lower the heat as needed. Sear and baste the steaks for about 3½ minutes on each side for medium-rare meat.
3. Remove the steaks from the pan and place on a cutting board. Allow to rest for at least 5 minutes before slicing and serving. Discard the rosemary and garlic.

PER SERVING:
CALORIES 350 | **PROTEIN** 34.4g | **CARBS** 1.7g | **SUGARS** 0g | **FIBER** 0.5g | **FAT** 22.7g

GRILLED ELK
Carne Asada

YIELD: 4 servings | **PREP TIME:** 10 minutes, plus 1 hour to marinate steak (not including time to make dressing) | **COOK TIME:** 10 minutes

You can swap out the lettuce cups in this recipe for grain-free tortillas. Just soften them in a dry skillet for 20 seconds on each side before serving.

MARINADE:

⅓ cup extra-virgin olive oil

Juice of 2 limes

1 teaspoon grated orange zest

Juice of 1 orange

2 cloves garlic, minced

2 teaspoons ground cumin

1½ teaspoons Redmond Real Salt

1 teaspoon ancho chili powder

1 (1¼-pound) elk flank steak

FOR SERVING:

1 head butter lettuce

1 avocado, sliced

4 radishes, thinly sliced

1 cup grape tomatoes, halved

5 ounces Cotija cheese, grated

2 tablespoons fresh cilantro leaves

½ cup Avocado Lime Dressing (page 215)

4 lime wedges

1. Make the marinade: Whisk together the olive oil, lime juice, orange zest and juice, garlic, cumin, salt, and chili powder in a medium bowl.
2. Lay the flank steak flat in a glass or ceramic dish, then evenly coat both sides with the marinade. Cover and refrigerate for at least 1 hour or overnight.
3. Remove the steak from the refrigerator and discard the excess marinade.
4. Heat a grill to high heat. Grill the steak for 5 minutes on each side, until cooked to medium-rare.
5. Remove the steak from the grill and allow to rest for 10 minutes, then cut crosswise into thin slices.
6. Pull apart the lettuce leaves to make lettuce cups.
7. To serve, arrange the lettuce cups, avocado slices, radishes, tomatoes, cheese, cilantro leaves, dressing, and lime wedges on a platter. Serve alongside the meat for making build-your-own taco lettuce cups.
8. Store in an airtight container in the refrigerator for up to 3 days.

PER SERVING:
CALORIES 719 | **PROTEIN** 49.9g | **CARBS** 16.7g | **SUGARS** 4.9g | **FIBER** 6.1g | **FAT** 42.9g

PEPPERCORN-CRUSTED *Elk Tenderloin*

YIELD: 4 servings | **PREP TIME:** 5 minutes (not including time to make sauce)
COOK TIME: 14 minutes

This dish pairs well with Hasselback Sweet Potatoes with Maple Bacon Butter (page 159).

1¼ pounds elk tenderloin

¼ cup Dijon mustard

¾ teaspoon Redmond Real Salt

1 tablespoon plus 1 teaspoon mixed peppercorns, crushed

1 cup High-Protein Horseradish Sauce (page 219), for serving

1. Preheat the oven to 425°F.
2. Pat the elk tenderloin dry with a paper towel. Brush the meat with the mustard, coating it evenly. Coat the tenderloin evenly with the salt and crushed peppercorns, pressing the pepper into the meat to form a secure coating.
3. Put the tenderloin in a roasting pan and roast for 12 to 14 minutes, until the internal temperature is 125°F to 130°F.
4. Remove from the oven and transfer the tenderloin to a cutting board. Allow to rest for at least 5 minutes before slicing. Cut into ½-inch-thick slices and serve with the horseradish sauce.

Note: Whole elk tenderloin varies greatly in size. You may have to buy two small tenderloins, or buy one larger one and cut off the excess and save it for another meal. Or cook it all! This recipe is easy to scale up or down, depending on what you can find. The cook time will vary according to the size you find; just go by the internal temperature to ensure that you end up with perfectly cooked meat.

PER SERVING:
CALORIES 340 | **PROTEIN** 40g | **CARBS** 4g | **SUGARS** 1g | **FIBER** 1g | **FAT** 12g

SEAFOOD

PORCHETTA *Salmon*

YIELD: 2 servings | **PREP TIME:** 4 minutes, plus 1 hour to marinate (not including time to make salt rub) | **COOK TIME:** 10 minutes

When sourcing salmon, always look for wild-caught Alaskan varieties like sockeye, king, or Chinook. Alaskan salmon has a short season that lasts from June through September, but it can be purchased frozen during the other months of the year.

2 (6-ounce) skin-on wild-caught Alaskan salmon fillets

2 tablespoons Porchetta Salt Rub (page 224)

1 tablespoon avocado oil

2 lemon wedges, for serving

1. Pat the salmon fillets dry with a paper towel. Press the salt rub into the flesh side of the salmon. Cover and refrigerate for at least 1 hour or overnight.
2. Preheat the oven to 425°F.
3. Remove the salmon from the refrigerator 10 minutes before cooking. Brush the salmon fillets on both sides with the avocado oil and place in a medium ovenproof skillet.
4. Bake for 10 minutes, or until cooked to medium-rare. Allow to rest for 5 minutes before serving.
5. To serve, squeeze the lemon juice on the fillets.

PER SERVING:
CALORIES 306 | **PROTEIN** 25.3g | **CARBS** 3.4g | **SUGARS** 0.6g | **FIBER** 0.3g | **FAT** 21g

HOT HONEY Salmon Bites

YIELD: 2 servings | **PREP TIME:** 6 minutes, plus 1 hour to marinate fish
COOK TIME: 6 minutes

Try serving these salmon bites with sheets of nori (sometimes labeled as "sushi nori"). You can roll the nori into a cone shape, pop the salmon inside, and eat it with your hands.

HOT HONEY SAUCE:

2 tablespoons avocado oil mayonnaise

1 tablespoons Sriracha sauce

1 tablespoon honey

½ teaspoon red miso paste

Juice of ½ lime

1 (12-ounce) skin-on wild-caught Alaskan salmon fillet

FOR GARNISH:

2 scallions, chopped

1 teaspoon mixed black and white sesame seeds

4 lime wedges

1. Make the hot honey sauce: Whisk together the mayonnaise, Sriracha, honey, miso, and lime juice in a small bowl.
2. Cut the salmon into 2-inch strips. Pat dry with a paper towel. Brush generously with the hot honey sauce. Arrange on a parchment-lined sheet pan or air fryer tray and refrigerate for 1 hour.
3. Preheat the oven or an air fryer to 425°F.
4. Remove the salmon from the refrigerator 10 minutes before cooking.
5. Roast or air-fry the fish for 5 to 6 minutes, until cooked to medium-rare.
6. Let rest for 3 minutes. Garnish with the scallions, sesame seeds, and lime wedges and serve.

PER SERVING:
CALORIES 394 | **PROTEIN** 25.6g | **CARBS** 14.2g | **SUGARS** 10.1g | **FIBER** 0.7g | **FAT** 25.8g

QUINOA-CRUSTED FISH STICKS
with Lemon Dill Sauce

YIELD: 4 servings | **PREP TIME:** 16 minutes (not including time to make salt or sauce)
COOK TIME: 8 minutes

Here, as in the Chicken Parm recipe on page 73, quinoa flakes are the perfect substitute for breadcrumbs. For a spicier breading, you can add another teaspoon of Chile Lime Salt Rub.

1 pound firm white fish fillets, such as cod or halibut

½ teaspoon Redmond Real Salt

½ cup arrowroot starch

2 large eggs

¾ cup quinoa flakes

½ teaspoon Chile Lime Salt Rub (page 223)

2 tablespoons avocado oil

FOR SERVING:

¾ cup Lemon Dill Sauce (page 220)

4 lemon wedges

1. Preheat the oven or an air fryer to 400°F. Line a sheet pan or the air fryer tray with parchment paper.
2. Cut the fish into 3-inch-long strips that are ½ inch wide and ½ inch thick. Pat the fish sticks dry with a paper towel, then season with the salt.
3. Put the arrowroot in a shallow bowl.
4. Whisk the eggs in a medium bowl.
5. Whisk together the quinoa flakes and salt rub in another medium bowl.
6. Dredge the fish sticks one at a time in the arrowroot, shaking off any excess. Dip into the eggs and then into the quinoa mixture. Make sure each stick is evenly coated.
7. Arrange the breaded fish sticks on the prepared pan or tray, spreading out evenly and leaving space between them. (If using the smaller air fryer tray, you will need to cook the fish sticks in two batches to avoid crowding.) Bake or air-fry for 8 minutes, or until crispy. Turn the fish over after 4 minutes to make sure all sides turn golden brown and crispy.
8. Let rest for 3 minutes before serving with the Lemon Dill Sauce and lemon wedges.

PER SERVING:
CALORIES 349 | **PROTEIN** 30.1g | **CARBS** 27.1g | **SUGARS** 1.3g | **FIBER** 1.8g | **FAT** 13g

GRILLED MAHI FISH TACOS
with Pink Pineapple Salsa

YIELD: 2 servings | **PREP TIME:** 10 minutes | **COOK TIME:** 9 minutes

If you can't find mahi mahi, try any firm fish, like halibut, cod, or salmon. The salsa can be made up to a day in advance. If you prefer a spicy salsa, leave the ribs and seeds in the jalapeño.

PINEAPPLE SALSA:

1½ cups diced pineapple

2 tablespoons finely diced red onions

⅛ teaspoon grated lime zest

Juice of 1 lime

1 teaspoon finely diced deveined and seeded jalapeño pepper

TACOS:

12 ounces mahi mahi fillets

2 tablespoons avocado oil

½ teaspoon Redmond Real Salt

⅛ teaspoon cracked black pepper

4 (6-inch) grain-free tortillas

1 Persian or other small seedless cucumber, thinly sliced

¼ cup thinly sliced red onions

1 tablespoon fresh cilantro leaves

4 lime wedges, for serving

1. Make the salsa: Mix together the pineapple, onions, lime zest and juice, and jalapeño in a medium bowl. Cover and refrigerate until ready to serve.
2. Preheat a grill or grill pan on the stovetop to medium-high heat.
3. Cut the mahi mahi into 4 equal pieces. Brush evenly with the avocado oil and season with the salt and pepper.
4. Grill the fish until it releases easily with a spatula and has distinct grill marks, about 4 minutes. Carefully turn the fish over and grill for another 4 minutes, or until the fish is firm to the touch. Remove from the heat and allow to rest for 5 minutes.
5. Grill the tortillas for 20 seconds on each side, until softened.
6. To assemble the tacos, fill the tortillas with the fish, cucumber, sliced onions, and cilantro and top with the pineapple salsa. Serve with the lime wedges.

PER SERVING:
CALORIES 300 | **PROTEIN** 30g | **CARBS** 40g | **SUGARS** 10g | **FIBER** 5g | **FAT** 25g

GINGER LIME *Whole Roasted Snapper*

YIELD: 2 servings | **PREP TIME:** 12 minutes, plus 1 hour to marinate | **COOK TIME:** 11 minutes

This recipe works well with other smaller whole fish like largemouth bass (aka black bass), branzino, porgy, or pompano. Try playing around with different fresh herbs inside the fish cavity, like cilantro or tarragon.

¼ cup tamari

¼ cup lime juice

3 tablespoons extra-virgin olive oil

1 (2-inch) knob ginger, grated

3 cloves garlic, minced

1 (2-pound) whole snapper (head on), scaled and cleaned

1 teaspoon Redmond Real Salt

2 limes, sliced into ¼-inch-thick rounds

8 large fresh basil leaves

1 tablespoon avocado oil

1. Make the marinade: Whisk together the tamari, lime juice, olive oil, ginger, and garlic in a small bowl.
2. Pat the fish dry with a paper towel. Score the fish twice on each side. Season inside and out with the salt. Stuff half of the lime slices and half of the basil leaves inside the fish cavity. Baste the outside of the fish with the marinade. Cover and refrigerate for 1 hour.
3. Preheat the oven to 425°F.
4. Heat the avocado oil in a large cast-iron skillet over medium heat. Once hot, place the fish in the pan and sear until golden brown, about 3 minutes. Turn the fish over, place the pan in the oven, and cook for an additional 6 to 8 minutes, until fully opaque in the center.
5. Remove the fish from the oven and allow to rest for 5 minutes.
6. To serve, fillet the fish and serve with the remaining lime slices and basil leaves.

PER SERVING:
CALORIES 480 | **PROTEIN** 45g | **CARBS** 7g | **SUGARS** 1g | **FIBER** 1g | **FAT** 25g

CEDAR PLANK EVERYTHING BAGEL SALT-CRUSTED TROUT
with Pickles & Lemon Dill Sauce

YIELD: 2 servings | **PREP TIME:** 8 minutes (not including time to make salt rub or sauce)
COOK TIME: 12 minutes

Can a fish dish remind you of an everything bagel with smoked salmon and cream cheese? This one sure can. As an alternative to the Lemon Dill Sauce, you can pair this fish with High-Protein Horseradish Sauce (page 219). Cooking it on a cedar plank imparts a woodsy flavor to the fish.

PICKLES:

2 Persian or other small seedless cucumbers, thinly sliced

2 tablespoons thinly sliced red onions

¼ cup apple cider vinegar

1 teaspoon Redmond Real Salt

FISH:

12 ounces ocean trout fillets (aka sea trout or steelhead trout), skin on

1 tablespoon Dijon mustard

3 tablespoons Everything Bagel Salt Rub (page 223)

½ cup Lemon Dill Sauce (page 220), for serving

Special equipment:

Cedar plank

1. Make the pickles: Put the cucumbers and onions in a jar with the vinegar and salt. Seal the lid and store in the refrigerator for up to 2 days.
2. Soak the cedar plank in water for 30 minutes.
3. Set up your grill for indirect heat so the plank doesn't burn. Preheat the grill to 350°F.
4. Pat the fish dry with a paper towel and place it skin side down on the cedar plank. Brush the fish with the mustard, then evenly crust the fish with the salt rub. Allow the fish to sit out at room temperature for 10 minutes.
5. Place the plank with the fish on the grill and cook for 10 to 12 minutes, until the fish reaches an internal temperature of 125°F. Remove from the grill and allow to rest for 5 minutes.
6. Serve the fish on the plank. Top with the pickles and set the sauce on the side.

PER SERVING:
CALORIES 450 | **PROTEIN** 30g | **CARBS** 10g | **SUGARS** 4g | **FIBER** 2g | **FAT** 30g

COCONUT-CRUSTED *Shrimp*

YIELD: 1 pound shrimp | **PREP TIME:** 10 minutes | **COOK TIME:** 12 minutes

When buying shrimp, always look for wild-caught as opposed to farm-raised. Try the Banh Mi Dressing (page 216) as a dipping sauce for this dish.

- 1 pound jumbo wild-caught shrimp, tails on
- ¼ teaspoon Redmond Real Salt
- ⅔ cup arrowroot starch
- 2 large eggs
- ¾ cup unsweetened shredded coconut
- 1 tablespoon extra-virgin olive oil

1. Preheat the oven or an air fryer to 350°F. Line a sheet pan or the air fryer tray with parchment paper.
2. Remove the shells from the shrimp, leaving the tails on. Devein the shrimp and butterfly them. Pat them dry with a paper towel. Season with the salt.
3. Create a dredging station: Put the arrowroot, eggs, and coconut in 3 separate medium bowls. Beat the eggs.
4. Dredge the shrimp in the arrowroot, then dip in the eggs and then the coconut, making sure the shrimp is completely coated. Place on the prepared pan or tray and brush with the olive oil.
5. Bake or air-fry for 12 minutes, or until the coconut is golden brown and the shrimp is cooked through and opaque. Serve immediately.

PER SERVING:
CALORIES 132 | **PROTEIN** 10.8g | **CARBS** 7.6g | **SUGARS** 0.7g | **FIBER** 1g | **FAT** 6.4g

MUSSELS *in Creamy Turmeric Broth*

YIELD: 4 servings | **PREP TIME:** 10 minutes | **COOK TIME:** 15 minutes

This one-pot dish is super easy to make. Although we like to use freshly grated turmeric in many of our recipes, here turmeric powder works best for the vibrant color it provides. Serve the mussels with a side of rice.

1 tablespoon extra-virgin olive oil

½ cup thinly sliced yellow onions

½ cup thinly sliced yellow bell peppers

½ cup thinly sliced red bell peppers

1 (1-inch) knob ginger, grated

2 cloves garlic, sliced

2 red Thai chile peppers, sliced into ½-inch sections

½ stalk lemongrass, outer leaves discarded, chopped

15 ounces fish stock or water

1 (14-ounce) can full-fat coconut milk

1 teaspoon fish sauce

1 teaspoon turmeric powder

4 pounds mussels, scrubbed

Juice of 1 lime

FOR GARNISH:

2 tablespoons fresh cilantro leaves

4 lime wedges

1. Heat the olive oil in a large saucepan over medium heat. When hot, add the onions and bell peppers and sauté until the onions are translucent, about 5 minutes.
2. Add the ginger, garlic, chiles, lemongrass, fish stock, coconut milk, fish sauce, and turmeric powder and bring to a boil.
3. Add the mussels, cover with a lid, and cook until the mussels open, about 6 minutes.
4. Remove the pot from the heat and stir in the lime juice.
5. To serve, garnish with the cilantro and lime wedges.

PER SERVING:
CALORIES 475 | **PROTEIN** 44.2g | **CARBS** 20.3g | **SUGARS** 4g | **FIBER** 1.5g | **FAT** 25g

VEGETABLE SIDES

HIGH-PROTEIN *Mashed Potatoes*

YIELD: 6 servings | **PREP TIME:** 15 minutes | **COOK TIME:** 20 minutes

Here, yogurt replaces the heavy cream used in most mashed potato recipes, reducing the calories and increasing the protein content. For a twist on the flavor, try mixing 2 tablespoons of Green Tahini Dressing (page 214) into these potatoes.

2 pounds large Yukon Gold potatoes

2 teaspoons Redmond Real Salt

⅓ cup chicken bone broth

¼ cup (½ stick) unsalted butter

¾ cup plain Greek yogurt (5% fat)

1 tablespoon finely chopped fresh chives, for garnish

1. Peel the potatoes and cut them into 2-inch cubes.
2. Put the potatoes in a large pot and cover with cold water. Set the pot over high heat and bring to a boil.
3. When the water reaches a boil, add the salt. Boil the potatoes until you can easily slide a knife through them, about 20 minutes.
4. While the potatoes are cooking, warm the broth and butter in a small saucepan over medium heat until the butter is melted. Set aside.
5. Drain the potatoes and transfer them to a stand mixer. Add the broth mixture and yogurt. Whip on medium-high speed until the potatoes are light and fluffy.
6. Top with the chives and serve. Store in an airtight container in the refrigerator for up to 3 days.

PER SERVING:
CALORIES 194 | **PROTEIN** 6.4g | **CARBS** 24.9g | **SUGARS** 1.6g | **FIBER** 2.4g | **FAT** 8.1g

CRISPY SMASHED *Yukon Golds*

YIELD: 6 servings | **PREP TIME:** 12 minutes | **COOK TIME:** 1 hour

These potatoes are a great accompaniment to any of the beef or poultry dishes in this cookbook. Or try them as a vehicle for dipping into any of the high-protein dressings and sauces on pages 208 to 225.

1 pound small Yukon Gold potatoes

2¾ teaspoons Redmond Real Salt, divided

2 tablespoons unsalted butter or duck fat, melted

1 tablespoon extra-virgin olive oil

½ teaspoon paprika

¼ teaspoon cracked black pepper

1 tablespoon chopped fresh Italian parsley, for garnish

1. Put the potatoes in a large pot and fill with cold water. Set the pot over high heat and bring to a boil.
2. When the water reaches a boil, add the salt. Boil the potatoes for 20 to 25 minutes, until you can easily slide a knife through them.
3. Drain the potatoes in a colander and let them rest for 5 minutes.
4. Preheat the oven to 425°F. Line a sheet pan with parchment paper.
5. Whisk together the butter, olive oil, paprika, pepper, and remaining ¾ teaspoon of salt.
6. Arrange the potatoes on the prepared pan. Using the bottom of a cup, smash each potato. Brush both sides of the potatoes with the butter mixture.
7. Bake for 30 to 35 minutes, until the desired level of crispiness is reached. Garnish with the parsley and serve immediately.

PER SERVING:
CALORIES 106 | **PROTEIN** 1.4g | **CARBS** 11.9g | **SUGARS** 0.3g | **FIBER** 1.3g | **FAT** 6.1g

HASSELBACK SWEET POTATOES
with Maple Bacon Butter

YIELD: 2 potatoes | **PREP TIME:** 12 minutes (not including time to cook bacon)
COOK TIME: 55 minutes

If you are new to making a Hasselback potato, you can prevent the knife from slicing all the way through the potato by setting two chopsticks on your cutting board parallel to one another, putting the potato between them, and then making crosswise slices.

- 2 sweet potatoes (about 7 ounces each), scrubbed
- 1 teaspoon extra-virgin olive oil
- ¼ teaspoon Redmond Real Salt
- 4 fresh sage leaves
- 2 teaspoons unsalted butter
- 2 teaspoons maple syrup
- 6 ounces bacon, cooked and chopped

1. Preheat the oven to 425°F. Line a sheet pan with parchment paper.
2. Make a series of ⅛-inch slices along each sweet potato, being sure to cut only two-thirds of the way through to the bottom of the potato.
3. Rub the potatoes all over with the oil, then season with the salt. Place on the prepared pan and top with the sage leaves. Bake for 50 minutes, or until the flesh is tender and the skins are crisp.
4. While the potatoes are in the oven, heat the butter and maple syrup in a small saucepan over medium heat. Once the butter is melted, stir in the bacon. Remove from the heat and set aside.
5. Remove the potatoes from the oven. Run a fork over the tops of the potatoes, fanning them out.
6. Spoon the maple bacon butter over the potatoes, being sure to get it in between the slices.
7. Return the potatoes to the oven for 5 minutes, allowing them to caramelize. Serve immediately.

PER SERVING:
CALORIES 400 | **PROTEIN** 9g | **CARBS** 50g | **SUGARS** 15g | **FIBER** 6g | **FAT** 20g

SWEET POTATO *Fries*

YIELD: 2 servings | **PREP TIME:** 10 minutes | **COOK TIME:** 20 minutes

Making these fries in an air fryer gives them the closest texture to deep-frying. Tired of ketchup? Try serving these fries with High-Protein Jalapeno Ranch Dressing (page 218) or Turmeric Tahini Dressing (page 213).

- 1 pound sweet potatoes
- ¼ teaspoon Redmond Real Salt
- ¼ teaspoon garlic powder
- ¼ teaspoon smoked paprika
- 1 tablespoon extra-virgin olive oil

1. Preheat an air fryer or the oven to 400°F. Line the air fryer tray or a sheet pan with parchment paper.
2. Peel the sweet potatoes, or leave the skins on if you prefer. Cut the potatoes lengthwise into ½-inch wedges.
3. Toss the potatoes in a medium bowl with the salt, garlic powder, paprika, and olive oil.
4. Spread the wedges evenly on the prepared tray or sheet pan so they're not touching. (You may need to work in batches if using an air fryer, depending on the size of your air fryer.) Bake for 20 minutes, or according to the directions of your air fryer, until golden brown and cooked through.
5. Serve immediately.

PER SERVING:
CALORIES 257 | **PROTEIN** 3.6g | **CARBS** 45.5g | **SUGARS** 8g | **FIBER** 6.6g | **FAT** 7.3g

BROCCOLI STEM *Slaw*

YIELD: 4 servings | **PREP TIME:** 12 minutes, plus 1 hour to chill (not including time to make dressing)

Broccoli stems are often discarded. But if you peel their tough outer skin, you find a delicious prebiotic part of the broccoli that can be enjoyed either raw or cooked. The stems are rich in fiber.

2 cups peeled and julienned broccoli stems (from 2 heads)

1 cup julienned carrots

1 cup shaved red cabbage

¼ cup thinly sliced red onions

1 Granny Smith apple, julienned (do not peel)

¾ teaspoon Redmond Real Salt

1 cup High-Protein Jalapeño Ranch Dressing (page 218)

1. Combine the broccoli stems, carrots, cabbage, onions, and apple in a large bowl. Season with the salt.
2. Add the dressing and toss until evenly coated.
3. Refrigerate for at least 1 hour before serving. The slaw will keep for up to 3 days.

PER SERVING:
CALORIES 219 | **PROTEIN** 2.8g | **CARBS** 16.1g | **SUGARS** 7.9g | **FIBER** 3.9g | **FAT** 16.3g

BRUSSELS SPROUT *Slaw*

YIELD: 4 servings | **PREP TIME:** 12 minutes, plus 1 hour to chill

Want to make a full meal out of this slaw? Top it with a couple of jammy farm-fresh eggs, following the cooking method in the recipe for Asparagus with Jammy Eggs on page 179.

LEMON DRESSING:

2 teaspoons Dijon mustard

2 teaspoons honey

½ teaspoon fresh thyme leaves

¼ teaspoon grated lemon zest

¼ cup lemon juice

½ cup extra-virgin olive oil

¼ teaspoon Redmond Real Salt

¼ teaspoon cracked black pepper

SLAW:

1 pound Brussels sprouts

¼ red onion, thinly sliced

1 tablespoon chopped fresh Italian parsley

4 ounces Parmesan cheese, shaved, for garnish

1. Make the dressing: Whisk together the mustard, honey, thyme, lemon zest, and lemon juice in a medium bowl. While whisking, slowly stream in the olive oil until the dressing has emulsified. Set aside.
2. Thinly slice the Brussels sprouts on a mandoline. (If you don't have a mandoline, use a sharp chef's knife.)
3. Mix the shaved Brussels sprouts, onion slices, and parsley in a medium bowl.
4. Pour in the dressing and massage it into the Brussels mixture.
5. Refrigerate for at least 1 hour before serving. To plate, garnish with the shaved Parmesan.

PER SERVING:
CALORIES 419 | **PROTEIN** 13.3g | **CARBS** 14.9g | **SUGARS** 5.3g | **FIBER** 3.8g | **FAT** 35.6g

ROASTED BRUSSELS SPROUTS
with Ginger Miso Almond Butter Sauce

YIELD: 4 servings | **PREP TIME:** 5 minutes (not including time to make sauce)
COOK TIME: 25 minutes

The Ginger Miso Almond Butter Sauce featured in this recipe has so many uses. It started out as the base of Chicken Pad Thai (page 71), but it's also great as a dip, salad dressing, or coating for roasted Brussels sprouts (or any cooked vegetable).

1 pound large Brussels sprouts

2 tablespoons extra-virgin olive oil

½ teaspoon Redmond Real Salt

3 tablespoons Ginger Miso Almond Butter Sauce (page 208)

2 tablespoons sliced almonds, lightly toasted, for garnish

1. Preheat the oven to 400°F. Line a sheet pan with parchment paper.
2. Trim the bottoms off of the Brussels sprouts and remove any yellow outer leaves. Cut the sprouts in half through the stem.
3. Toss the Brussels sprouts with the olive oil and salt in a medium bowl.
4. Spread the sprouts evenly on the prepared pan. Roast for 20 to 25 minutes, until browned.
5. Remove from the oven and toss in a bowl with the sauce. To serve, garnish with the toasted almonds.
6. Store in an airtight container in the refrigerator for up to 3 days.

PER SERVING:
CALORIES 162 | **PROTEIN** 4.6g | **CARBS** 10.9g | **SUGARS** 2.3g | **FIBER** 4.3g | **FAT** 12.3g

CHEDDAR

YIELD: 20 tots (5 per serving) | **PREP TIME:** 15 minutes | **COOK TIME:** 18 minutes

Tots aren't just for taters. You can also try this recipe with cauliflower or carrots.

1 tablespoon extra-virgin olive oil

½ cup finely diced yellow onions

1¾ teaspoons Redmond Real Salt, divided

8 ounces broccoli florets

1 cup shredded sharp cheddar cheese

2 large eggs

½ cup quinoa flakes

Pinch of ground white pepper

Dash of hot sauce

1. Preheat the oven or an air fryer to 400°F. Line a sheet pan or the air fryer tray with parchment paper.
2. Heat the olive oil in a small skillet over medium heat. Add the onions and sauté until translucent, about 4 minutes. Remove the pan from the heat. Set aside.
3. Bring a large pot of water to a boil over high heat. Add 1 teaspoon of the salt and the broccoli and cook until soft, about 2½ minutes.
4. Drain the broccoli and pat dry.
5. Put the sautéed onions, broccoli, remaining ¾ teaspoon of salt, cheddar, eggs, quinoa flakes, pepper, and hot sauce in a food processor. Pulse until the ingredients are combined but the mixture remains chunky.
6. Using a 1-tablespoon cookie scoop, scoop out tots onto the prepared pan, spacing them evenly. (You should have about 20 tots.) Pat them down on the top to shape like a mini burger.
7. Bake or air-fry for 12 minutes, or according to the instructions for your air fryer, until the tots are golden brown. If using an air fryer, you may need to work in batches depending on the size of your air fryer.
8. Serve immediately.

PER SERVING:
CALORIES 49 | **PROTEIN** 2.7g | **CARBS** 2.5g | **SUGARS** 0.4g | **FIBER** 0.5g | **FAT** 3.2g

ZUCCHINI FRITTERS
with Lemon Yogurt Sauce

YIELD: 12 fritters (3 per serving) | **PREP TIME:** 20 minutes | **COOK TIME:** 12 minutes

When frying these fritters, mixing olive oil and butter creates a higher smoke point, preventing the butter from browning too quickly.

LEMON YOGURT SAUCE:

½ cup plain Greek yogurt (5% fat)

⅛ teaspoon grated lemon zest

Juice of ½ lemon

⅛ teaspoon cracked black pepper

Pinch of Redmond Real Salt

Dash of hot sauce

ZUCCHINI FRITTERS:

1 pound zucchini

¾ teaspoon Redmond Real Salt

¾ cup chopped scallions

1 large egg, beaten

½ cup gluten-free oat flour

½ teaspoon baking powder

¼ teaspoon cracked black pepper

Pinch of fresh grated nutmeg

1 teaspoon extra-virgin olive oil, divided

1 teaspoon unsalted butter, divided

1. In a small bowl, mix together the ingredients for the sauce. Cover and refrigerate until ready to use. (The sauce can be made up to 3 days ahead.)
2. Wash the zucchini and trim off the ends. Grate the zucchini on the large holes of a box grater.
3. Put the grated zucchini in a large bowl and toss with the salt. Let sit for 15 minutes. Place the zucchini in a piece of cheesecloth or a clean kitchen towel and wring out the excess water.
4. Transfer the zucchini to a medium bowl. Add the scallions, egg, oat flour, baking powder, pepper, and nutmeg and stir until thoroughly combined.
5. Heat a large nonstick skillet over medium heat. Pour in ½ teaspoon of the olive oil and add ½ teaspoon of the butter. Swirl the pan to evenly coat the bottom.
6. Using a 1-tablespoon cookie scoop, scoop out six tightly packed fritters. When adding them to the pan, flatten the tops to give them a 1½-inch round shape. Brown for about 3 minutes on each side, until golden brown.
7. Repeat Steps 5 and 6 with the remaining batter, making a total of 12 fritters.
8. Serve immediately with the sauce.

PER SERVING:

CALORIES 45 | **PROTEIN** 2.8g | **CARBS** 5.5g | **SUGARS** 1.6g | **FIBER** 0.9g | **FAT** 2.1g

GREEN BEANS *with Kale Pesto & Blistered Tomatoes*

YIELD: 4 servings | **PREP TIME:** 10 minutes (not including time to make pesto)
COOK TIME: 11 minutes

This tasty side pairs well with just about any of the protein dishes in this book. To change it up, try swapping asparagus for the green beans.

1 pound green beans, trimmed

1 teaspoon Redmond Real Salt

1 cup grape tomatoes

1 tablespoon extra-virgin olive oil

2 sprigs fresh thyme

⅓ cup Miso Walnut Kale Pesto (page 209)

2 teaspoons chopped raw walnuts

1. Bring a large pot of water to a boil.
2. Prepare a medium bowl of ice water.
3. Add the green beans and salt to the boiling water and cook for 3 minutes, or until the beans are bright green but still crunchy. Remove the beans with a slotted spoon and submerge in the ice water. Allow to cool completely, then drain and set aside.
4. Preheat the oven to 400°F. Line a sheet pan with parchment paper.
5. Cut the tomatoes in half lengthwise, place in a medium bowl, and toss with the olive oil. Spread the tomatoes on the prepared pan and top with the thyme sprigs.
6. Roast for 8 minutes, or until the tomatoes are slightly blistered. Remove from the oven and set aside.
7. Toss the green beans with the pesto in a medium bowl.
8. Plate the green beans. Top with the tomatoes and walnuts and serve.

PER SERVING:
CALORIES 127 | **PROTEIN** 3.3g | **CARBS** 12.3g | **SUGARS** 3.1g | **FIBER** 5.2g | **FAT** 8.3g

SAUTÉED

YIELD: 2 servings | **PREP TIME:** 8 minutes | **COOK TIME:** 5 minutes

Don't discard the stems of the chard! They are full of color, flavor, texture, and prebiotic fiber. Just cook them before adding the greens.

1 bunch rainbow chard

2 tablespoons extra-virgin olive oil

2 large cloves garlic, thinly sliced

¼ teaspoon Redmond Real Salt

½ lemon

1. Cut the stems off the chard and cut them into small dice, about ¼ inch. Slice the chard leaves into 2-inch ribbons.
2. Heat a large skillet over medium heat. Pour in the olive oil, then add the diced chard stems and garlic. Sauté until translucent, about 3 minutes.
3. Add the chard leaf ribbons and cook, stirring occasionally, until the leaves are tender, about 2 minutes.
4. Remove the pan from the heat and season the greens with the salt. Squeeze the lemon over the greens. Serve immediately.

PER SERVING:
CALORIES 147 | **PROTEIN** 1.9g | **CARBS** 5.7g | **SUGARS** 1.3g | **FIBER** 1.7g | **FAT** 13.5g

CHICORY SALAD *with Figs*

YIELD: 2 servings | **PREP TIME:** 10 minutes

This signature lettuce mix of greens from the chicory family can be paired with just about any dish. You can mix the greens in advance and store them on top of a paper towel in an airtight container in the refrigerator for up to 5 days. Fig balsamic vinegar is an amazing-tasting vinegar that can be used in many salads. It works really well when you're putting steak over salad.

6 fresh black Mission figs

½ small fennel bulb

1 cup torn frisée lettuce, escarole, or endive

1 cup baby spinach

1 small head radicchio, leaves picked

5 fresh basil leaves

1 tablespoon fresh Italian parsley leaves

1 tablespoon finely chopped fresh chives

¼ cup thinly sliced red onions

1½ tablespoons extra-virgin olive oil

1 tablespoon fig balsamic vinegar

¼ teaspoon Redmond Real Salt

⅛ teaspoon cracked black pepper

1. Cut the figs in half and set aside.
2. Prepare a medium bowl of ice water. Thinly slice the fennel on a mandoline. (If you don't have a mandoline, use a sharp chef's knife.) Submerge the fennel in the ice water for about 10 minutes. Drain the fennel and pat dry.
3. Mix the fennel, frisée, spinach, radicchio, basil, parsley, chives, and onion slices in a large salad bowl. Drizzle the olive oil and vinegar over the salad greens. Season with the salt and pepper and toss well.
4. To serve, top with the figs.

Note: The salad mixture can be made up to 2 days in advance. Dress with the oil and vinegar when ready to serve.

PER SERVING:
CALORIES 233 | **PROTEIN** 3.1g | **CARBS** 27.9g | **SUGARS** 19g | **FIBER** 6.1g | **FAT** 14.2g

ASPARAGUS with Jammy Eggs

YIELD: 2 servings | **PREP TIME:** 10 minutes | **COOK TIME:** 7 minutes

Once you perfect these precisely timed jammy eggs, you will be putting them on everything! Be sure to look for really good-quality organic eggs.

4 large eggs

1 bunch thick asparagus

2 tablespoons Redmond Real Salt

Juice of ½ lemon

1½ tablespoons extra-virgin olive oil

2 ounces Parmesan cheese, shaved

1 teaspoon chopped fresh chives

¼ teaspoon grated lemon zest

1. Prepare a medium bowl of ice water.
2. Bring a small saucepan of water to a rolling boil. Using a slotted spoon, carefully lower each egg into the water. Cook for 7 minutes.
3. Using the slotted spoon, remove the eggs and submerge them in the ice bath for 3 minutes. Peel the eggs and set aside.
4. Trim the asparagus, cutting off the woody bottoms of the stems. Using a vegetable peeler, peel the bottom 3 inches of each spear. Discard the peels.
5. Bring a large pot of water to a boil. Add the salt and asparagus and cook until the desired tenderness is reached; 3 minutes of cooking time should give you firm asparagus.
6. Remove the asparagus from the water and pat dry with a paper towel.
7. Drizzle the asparagus with the lemon juice and olive oil.
8. Cut the eggs in half and place on top of the asparagus. Sprinkle with the shaved Parmesan, chives and lemon zest.

PER SERVING:
CALORIES 411 | **PROTEIN** 26.2g | **CARBS** 9.7g | **SUGARS** 4.9g | **FIBER** 3.5g | **FAT** 30.8g

TURMERIC PICKLED *Cauliflower*

YIELD: 1 (750-ml) jar (4 servings) | **PREP TIME:** 5 minutes, plus 48 hours to pickle
COOK TIME: 5 minutes

If you want to play around with color, swap the turmeric root for 1 small, peeled beet and watch the cauliflower turn a vibrant pink hue.

- 4 (2-inch) pieces turmeric root
- 1¼ cups water
- ½ cup apple cider vinegar
- 2 teaspoons Redmond Real Salt
- 1 tablespoon sugar
- ¼ red onion, thinly sliced
- 12 ounces cauliflower florets
- 2 bay leaves
- 1 teaspoon black peppercorns
- 1 teaspoon mustard seeds

1. Peel the turmeric root and cut into matchsticks. Set aside.
2. Bring the water, vinegar, and salt to a boil in a small saucepan. Remove from the heat and stir in the sugar until dissolved. Set aside.
3. Put the onion slices in a wide-mouth 750-ml jar. Add the cauliflower florets, turmeric, bay leaves, peppercorns, and mustard seeds.
4. Pour the vinegar mixture over the cauliflower mixture, covering it completely. Set aside until fully cool.
5. Secure the lid on the jar and refrigerate for up to 3 weeks. The pickles will be ready in 48 hours but will taste better the longer they stay in the brine.

PER SERVING:
CALORIES 48 | **PROTEIN** 2.3g | **CARBS** 9.9g | **SUGARS** 5.3g | **FIBER** 3.2g | **FAT** 0.6g

CORIANDER PICKLED *Baby Carrots*

YIELD: 1 (750-ml) jar (4 servings) | **PREP TIME:** 5 minutes, plus 48 hours to pickle
COOK TIME: 5 minutes

You can spice up these carrots by adding a sliced serrano pepper to the mix or a jalapeño for even more heat.

1 cup water

½ cup apple cider vinegar

2 teaspoons Redmond Real Salt

1 tablespoon sugar

8 ounces baby carrots

3 cloves garlic, peeled

3 sprigs fresh cilantro

1 teaspoon black peppercorns

1 teaspoon coriander seeds

1. Bring the water, vinegar, and salt to a boil in a small saucepan. Remove from the heat and stir in the sugar until dissolved. Set aside.
2. Put the carrots in a wide-mouth 750-ml jar. Add the garlic, cilantro sprigs, peppercorns, and coriander seeds.
3. Pour the vinegar mixture over the carrot mixture, covering it completely. Set aside until fully cool.
4. Secure the lid on the jar and refrigerate for up to 3 weeks. The pickles will be ready in 48 hours but will taste better the longer they stay in the brine.

PER SERVING:
CALORIES 29 | **PROTEIN** 0.6g | **CARBS** 6.8g | **SUGARS** 4.3g | **FIBER** 1.1g | **FAT** 0.1g

PIZZA *and* FLATBREADS

PIZZA

YIELD: four 6½-inch crusts | **PREP TIME:** 10 minutes | **COOK TIME:** 6 minutes

This yeast-free recipe is much quicker to make than traditional pizza crust. For a softer crust, you can use low-fat Greek yogurt rather than nonfat. Want to add more fiber? Mix in 2 tablespoons of flax meal. If you want to get fancy with these crusts, you can crimp the dough all the way around to create a pretty edge.

- 1 cup nonfat plain Greek yogurt
- ¾ cup gluten-free oat flour, plus more for the work surface
- ¼ cup arrowroot starch
- 1½ teaspoons baking powder
- ½ teaspoon Redmond Real Salt
- 1 large egg, beaten

1. If using the oven, have one oven rack in the top third position and a second rack in the bottom third position. Preheat the oven or an air fryer to 400°F. Line two baking sheets or air fryer trays with parchment paper.
2. In a stand mixer fitted with the dough hook, knead the yogurt, oat flour, arrowroot, baking powder, and salt until a smooth ball has formed.
3. Dust your work surface with oat flour. Divide the dough into four equal portions, then roll each portion into a ball.
4. Dust the rolling pin with a small amount of oat flour, roll out each ball of dough into a circle, about 6½ inches in diameter. Place on the prepared pans, two dough circles per pan, and brush with the beaten egg.
5. Par-bake for 6 minutes, or until the crust is slightly golden. After 3 minutes, rotate and swap the pans.
6. Remove from the oven and use as the base for the pizza of your choice. The par-baked crusts can be stored in the refrigerator for up to three days.

Note: These par-baked crusts can be used to make any of the pizza recipes that follow or as the base for your own pizza creations. For the latter, after topping the crust with your favorite pizza toppings, return it to a preheated 400°F oven for about 6 minutes, or until the cheese is melted.

PER SERVING:
CALORIES 168 | **PROTEIN** 10.3g | **CARBS** 25.4g | **SUGARS** 2.2g | **FIBER** 2.5g | **FAT** 2.9g

PIZZA

YIELD: 4 individual pizzas | **PREP TIME:** 5 minutes (not including time to make par-baked crusts) | **COOK TIME:** 6 minutes

To put a new twist on this traditional favorite, try adding seasonal toppings, like squash blossoms during summer or shredded Brussels sprouts in the fall.

- 1 batch Pizza Crust (page 187)
- ½ cup no-sugar-added tomato sauce
- 1 cup shredded mozzarella cheese
- 2 teaspoons grated Parmesan cheese
- 6 fresh basil leaves, torn, for garnish

1. If using the oven, have one oven rack in the top third position and a second rack in the bottom third position. Preheat the oven or an air fryer to 400°F. Line two baking sheets or air fryer trays with parchment paper.
2. Place the par-baked pizza crusts on the prepared pans, two per pan.
3. Spread 2 tablespoons of tomato sauce on each crust. Sprinkle the mozzarella on the sauce, using about ¼ cup per pizza. Top with the Parmesan.
4. Bake for 6 minutes, or until the cheese is completely melted.
5. Remove from the oven and garnish with the torn basil leaves. Serve immediately.

Tip: The pizzas can be wrapped and stored in the freezer for up to 3 months.

PER SERVING:
CALORIES 271 | **PROTEIN** 17.7g | **CARBS** 28.1g | **SUGARS** 3.6g | **FIBER** 3g | **FAT** 10g

ARUGULA, PROSCIUTTO & RICOTTA *Pizza*

YIELD: 4 individual pizzas | **PREP TIME:** 5 minutes (not including time to make par-baked crusts) | **COOK TIME:** 6 minutes

You can get creative with the toppings for this white pizza. Try adding sliced fresh figs for a sweet and savory mix.

- 1 batch Pizza Crust (page 187)
- ¾ cup ricotta cheese
- ⅔ cup shredded mozzarella cheese
- 4 ounces sliced prosciutto
- 2 cups baby arugula
- 2 teaspoons extra-virgin olive oil
- 1 teaspoon balsamic vinegar
- Pinch of Redmond Real Salt

1. If using the oven, have one oven rack in the top third position and a second rack in the bottom third position. Preheat the oven or an air fryer to 400°F. Line two baking sheets or air fryer trays with parchment paper.
2. Place the par-baked pizza crusts on the prepared pans, two per pan.
3. Spoon the ricotta evenly over the crusts, then sprinkle the mozzarella evenly on the ricotta. Top with the prosciutto.
4. Bake for 6 minutes, or until the cheese is completely melted.
5. In a medium bowl, toss the arugula with the olive oil, vinegar, and salt.
6. To serve, top the pizzas with the dressed arugula.

PER SERVING:
CALORIES 408 | **PROTEIN** 26g | **CARBS** 30.2g | **SUGARS** 2.7g | **FIBER** 2.7g | **FAT** 20.4g

PEPPERONI & HOT HONEY *Pizza*

YIELD: 4 individual pizzas | **PREP TIME:** 5 minutes (not including time to make par-baked crusts) | **COOK TIME:** 6 minutes

Put a new spin on the classic pepperoni pizza by adding some trendy hot honey for a spicy-sweet kick. If you're not a fan of pepperoni, you can swap out your favorite salt-cured meat.

1 batch Pizza Crust (page 187)

½ cup no-sugar-added tomato sauce

1 cup shredded mozzarella cheese

4 ounces sliced pepperoni

2 teaspoons hot honey

1. If using the oven, have one oven rack in the top third position and a second rack in the bottom third position. Preheat the oven or an air fryer to 400°F. Line two baking sheets or air fryer trays with parchment paper.
2. Place the par-baked pizza crusts on the prepared pans, two per pan.
3. Spread 2 tablespoons of tomato sauce on each crust. Sprinkle the mozzarella evenly on the sauce. Top with the pepperoni.
4. Bake for 6 minutes, or until the cheese is completely melted.
5. Remove from the oven and drizzle with the hot honey. Serve immediately.

PER SERVING:
CALORIES 400 | **PROTEIN** 22.7g | **CARBS** 31.8g | **SUGARS** 6.3g | **FIBER** 3g | **FAT** 20.8g

FONTINA, MUSHROOM & SPINACH *Pizza*

YIELD: 4 individual pizzas | **PREP TIME:** 10 minutes (not including time to make par-baked crusts) | **COOK TIME:** 12 minutes

You can get creative with pizza flavors. Try swapping truffle cheese for the fontina.

1 batch Pizza Crust (page 187)

3 teaspoons extra-virgin olive oil, divided

½ cup sliced cremini mushrooms

½ teaspoon Redmond Real Salt, divided

3 cups baby spinach (packed)

1 cup shredded fontina cheese

1. If using the oven, have one oven rack in the top third position and a second rack in the bottom third position. Preheat the oven or an air fryer to 400°F. Line two baking sheets or air fryer trays with parchment paper.
2. Place the par-baked pizza crusts on the prepared pans, two per pan.
3. Heat 2 teaspoons of the olive oil in a medium skillet over high heat.
4. Add the mushrooms and sauté until browned, about 4 minutes. Season with ¼ teaspoon of the salt.
5. Remove the mushrooms from the pan and set aside.
6. Add the remaining teaspoon of olive oil to the skillet. Add the spinach, season with the remaining ¼ teaspoon of salt, and sauté until wilted, about 90 seconds. Slide the pan off the heat.
7. Sprinkle the crusts evenly with the cheese and top with the mushrooms and spinach.
8. Bake for 6 minutes, or until the cheese is completely melted. Serve immediately.

PER SERVING:

CALORIES 306 | **PROTEIN** 18.4g | **CARBS** 27.3g | **SUGARS** 2.6g | **FIBER** 3.2g | **FAT** 14.4g

FLATBREAD *Crust*

YIELD: four 8 by 3-inch par-baked crusts | **PREP TIME:** 10 minutes | **COOK TIME:** 6 minutes

The cottage cheese in this recipe helps give the flatbread a nice crisp texture and creates a platform for a lot of hearty toppings.

1 cup full-fat cottage cheese

¾ cup gluten-free oat flour, plus more for the work surface

¼ cup arrowroot starch

1½ teaspoons baking powder

½ teaspoon Redmond Real Salt

1 large egg, beaten

1. If using the oven, have one oven rack in the top third position and a second rack in the bottom third position. Preheat the oven or an air fryer to 400°F. Line two baking sheets or air fryer trays with parchment paper.
2. Blend the cottage cheese in a blender on high speed until smooth.
3. Spoon the cottage cheese into a stand mixer fitted with the dough hook. Add the oat flour, arrowroot, baking powder, and salt. Knead until a soft ball has formed.
4. Dust your work surface with oat flour. Divide the dough into four equal portions, then roll each portion into a smooth ball.
5. Using a rolling pin, roll out each ball of dough into a rectangle, about 8 by 3 inches. Place on the prepared pans, two per pan. Brush with the egg wash.
6. Par-bake for 6 minutes, or until slightly golden. Remove from the oven and use as the base for the flatbread of your choice.

Note: These par-baked flatbreads can be used to make any of the flatbread recipes in this book (see pages 198 to 205), or as the base for your own flatbread creations. For the latter, after topping the base with your favorite flatbread toppings, return it to a preheated 400°F oven for about 6 minutes, or until the cheese is melted.

PER SERVING:
CALORIES 185 | **PROTEIN** 11.6g | **CARBS** 25g | **SUGARS** 1.8g | **FIBER** 2.5g | **FAT** 4.9g

BUFFALO CHICKEN *Flatbreads*

YIELD: 4 individual flatbreads | **PREP TIME:** 8 minutes (not including time to make crust and sauce and cook chicken) | **COOK TIME:** 6 minutes

You can garnish this flatbread with crumbled blue cheese or a drizzle of High-Protein Jalapeño Ranch Dressing (page 218).

1 batch Flatbread Crust (page 197)

1 pound boneless, skinless chicken breasts, cooked and pulled

½ cup Buffalo Sauce (page 212)

½ cup no-sugar-added tomato sauce

1 cup shredded mozzarella cheese

1. If using the oven, have one oven rack in the top third position and a second rack in the bottom third position. Preheat the oven or an air fryer to 400°F. Line two baking sheets or air fryer trays with parchment paper.
2. Place the par-baked flatbread crusts on the prepared pans, two per pan.
3. Toss the chicken and buffalo sauce in a medium bowl until the chicken is evenly coated. Set aside.
4. Spread 2 tablespoons of tomato sauce on each flatbread crust. Then sprinkle evenly with the mozzarella. Top with the buffalo chicken mixture.
5. Bake for 6 minutes, or until the cheese is completely melted. Serve immediately.

PER SERVING:
CALORIES 491 | **PROTEIN** 51.9g | **CARBS** 26.2g | **SUGARS** 3.4g | **FIBER** 2.5g | **FAT** 18.9g

SOPRESSATA & OLIVE *Flatbreads*

YIELD: 4 individual flatbreads | **PREP TIME:** 5 minutes (not including time to make crust)
COOK TIME: 6 minutes

Want to add some sweetness to this recipe? Drizzle with aged balsamic vinegar.

1 batch Flatbread Crust (page 197)

½ cup no-sugar-added tomato sauce

1 cup shredded mozzarella cheese

4 ounces sliced sopressata

¼ cup pitted Kalamata olives, halved

1. If using the oven, have one oven rack in the top third position and a second rack in the bottom third position. Preheat the oven or an air fryer to 400°F. Line two baking sheets or air fryer trays with parchment paper.
2. Place the par-baked flatbread crusts on the prepared pans, two per pan.
3. Spread 2 tablespoons of tomato sauce on each flatbread crust. Sprinkle evenly with the mozzarella. Top with the sopressata slices and olives.
4. Bake for 6 minutes, or until the cheese is completely melted. Serve immediately.

PER SERVING:
CALORIES 399 | **PROTEIN** 23g | **CARBS** 26.2g | **SUGARS** 3.4g | **FIBER** 2.8g | **FAT** 23g

VEGGIE Flatbreads

YIELD: 4 individual flatbreads | **PREP TIME:** 8 minutes (not including time to make crust)
COOK TIME: 10 minutes

Calabrian chiles are a great way to add subtle heat to any dish. Choose the jarred ones that are preserved in olive oil.

- 1 batch Flatbread Crust (page 197)
- 1 tablespoon extra-virgin olive oil
- 1 zucchini, sliced into ⅛-inch rounds
- Pinch of Redmond Real Salt
- ½ cup no-sugar-added tomato sauce
- 1 cup shredded mozzarella cheese
- 6 marinated artichokes, quartered
- ½ cup grape tomatoes, halved
- ¼ small red onion, thinly sliced
- 4 jarred Calabrian chiles, chopped

1. If using the oven, have one oven rack in the top third position and a second rack in the bottom third position. Preheat the oven or an air fryer to 400°F. Line two baking sheets or air fryer trays with parchment paper.
2. Place the par-baked flatbread crusts on the prepared pans, two per pan.
3. Heat the olive oil in a large skillet over medium heat. Add the zucchini, season with the salt, and sauté on each side for 2 minutes. Remove from the heat. Set aside.
4. Spread 2 tablespoons of tomato sauce on each flatbread crust. Then sprinkle evenly with the mozzarella. Top with the zucchini, artichokes, tomatoes, onion slices, and chiles.
5. Bake for 6 minutes, or until the cheese is completely melted. Serve immediately.

PER SERVING:
CALORIES 339 | **PROTEIN** 18.4g | **CARBS** 30.9g | **SUGARS** 6.7g | **FIBER** 4.5g | **FAT** 16.5g

MEATY

YIELD: 4 individual flatbreads | **PREP TIME:** 8 minutes (not including time to make crust)
COOK TIME: 10 minutes

You can experiment with your favorite meats on this one—ground beef, bison, turkey, you name it!

- 1 batch Flatbread Crust (page 197)
- 1 pound gluten-free pork sage sausages
- 1 tablespoon extra-virgin olive oil
- ½ cup no-sugar-added tomato sauce
- 1 cup shredded mozzarella cheese

1. If using the oven, have one oven rack in the top third position and a second rack in the bottom third position. Preheat the oven or an air fryer to 400°F. Line two baking sheets or air fryer trays with parchment paper.
2. Place the par-baked flatbread crusts on the prepared pans, two per pan.
3. Remove the sausage meat from the casings. Discard the casings.
4. Heat the olive oil in a medium skillet over medium-high heat. Add the sausage and cook, stirring often to break it up, until evenly browned, about 5 minutes.
5. Spread 2 tablespoons of tomato sauce on each flatbread crust. Then sprinkle evenly with the mozzarella. Top with the browned sausage.
6. Bake for 6 minutes, or until the cheese is completely melted. Serve immediately.

PER SERVING:
CALORIES 633 | **PROTEIN** 34.9g | **CARBS** 26.2g | **SUGARS** 3.4g | **FIBER** 2.5g | **FAT** 43.7g

DRESSINGS *and* SAUCES

GINGER MISO
Almond Butter Sauce

YIELD: 1 cup (1 tablespoon per serving) | **PREP TIME:** 5 minutes

In addition to being a key component of Pad Thai, this thick, flavorful sauce makes a great dip, salad dressing, or topping for cooked vegetables.

- ¼ cup creamy raw almond butter
- 2 tablespoons lime juice
- 2 tablespoons red miso paste
- 2 tablespoons tamari
- 1 tablespoon maple syrup
- 1 tablespoon untoasted sesame oil
- 1 tablespoon grated fresh ginger
- 2 cloves garlic, peeled
- ¼ cup water, plus more if needed

1. Put all of the ingredients in a blender and blend on high speed until smooth and creamy. Add more water as needed to achieve the desired consistency.
2. Store in an airtight container in the refrigerator for up to 2 weeks.

PER SERVING:
CALORIES 43 | **PROTEIN** 1.2g | **CARBS** 2.7g | **SUGARS** 1.1g | **FIBER** 0.5g | **FAT** 3.3g

MISO WALNUT *Kale Pesto*

YIELD: 1½ cups (1 tablespoon per serving) | **PREP TIME:** 12 minutes
COOK TIME: 90 seconds

This pesto replaces Parmesan with miso, making it a dairy-free version. Miso imparts the same umami quality that Parmesan does. Use this pesto as a dip or as a sauce for cooked vegetables and on a pasta alternative like spaghetti squash.

2 cups stemmed curly kale leaves

¼ cup raw walnuts

1½ tablespoons white miso paste

2 cloves garlic, peeled

¼ teaspoon Redmond Real Salt

¼ cup extra-virgin olive oil

¼ cup water, plus more if needed

1. Bring a medium pot of salted water to a boil over high heat. Prepare a medium bowl of ice water.
2. Blanch the kale in the boiling water for 90 seconds. Remove the kale and submerge in the ice water; allow it to cool completely, about 3 minutes. Drain the kale and squeeze out any excess water.
3. Put the kale, walnuts, miso, garlic, and salt in a food processor. Pulse until the ingredients are combined and the mixture is chunky.
4. Stream in the olive oil while the food processor is running. Add the water and pulse to combine; add more water as needed to achieve the desired consistency.
5. Store in an airtight container in the refrigerator for up to a week.

PER SERVING:
CALORIES 31 | **PROTEIN** 0.4g | **CARBS** 0.6g | **SUGARS** 0.2g | **FIBER** 0.2g | **FAT** 3.1g

JAPANESE-STYLE BBQ *Sauce*

YIELD: 1½ cups (1 tablespoon per serving) | **PREP TIME:** 5 minutes | **COOK TIME:** 20 minutes

This sauce is a key ingredient in the chicken wing recipe on page 75. Also try switching up flavors in the turkey meatloaf recipe on page 81 by using it in place of the traditional BBQ sauce.

1 cup tamari

¼ cup maple syrup

2 tablespoons mirin

2 tablespoons tomato paste

1 tablespoon rice wine vinegar

1 tablespoon untoasted sesame oil

1 tablespoon grated fresh ginger

1 teaspoon minced garlic

½ teaspoon Redmond Real Salt

1. Put all of the ingredients in a medium saucepan and bring to a boil over medium heat.
2. Lower the heat to a simmer and continue to cook for 15 minutes, until thickened.
3. Allow the sauce to cool, then strain it.
4. Store in an airtight jar in the refrigerator for up to a month.

PER SERVING:
CALORIES 41 | **PROTEIN** 1.6g | **CARBS** 6.2g | **SUGARS** 4.4g | **FIBER** 0.1g | **FAT** 0.9g

BBQ

YIELD: 1 cup (¼ cup per serving) | PREP TIME: 5 minutes | COOK TIME: 25 minutes

Use this classic sauce to make BBQ Turkey Meatloaf (page 81). It also works well when you brush it on roasted salmon or chicken before and after roasting.

- 2 teaspoons avocado oil
- ½ cup diced yellow onions
- 1 clove garlic, minced
- ½ cup no-sugar-added tomato sauce
- ½ cup water
- ¼ cup maple syrup
- 2 tablespoons apple cider vinegar
- 1 teaspoon tamari
- ½ teaspoon Redmond Real Salt
- ½ teaspoon smoked paprika
- Pinch of cayenne pepper

1. Heat the avocado oil in a medium saucepan over medium heat. Add the onions and sauté until they start to caramelize, about 10 minutes.
2. Add the garlic, tomato sauce, water, maple syrup, vinegar, tamari, salt, smoked paprika, and cayenne to the pan and stir to combine.
3. Bring to a boil, then simmer for 12 minutes, until fully cooked. Remove the pan from the heat and allow to cool.
4. Transfer the mixture to a blender and blend on high speed until smooth.
5. Store in an airtight jar in the refrigerator for up to a month.

PER SERVING:
CALORIES 91 | PROTEIN 0.9g | CARBS 17.5g | SUGARS 15.3g | FIBER 0.9g | FAT 2.3g

BUFFALO *Sauce*

YIELD: 1 cup (1 tablespoon per serving) | **PREP TIME:** 5 minutes

Use this sauce to make Buffalo Chicken Salad (page 69) and Buffalo Chicken Flatbreads (page 199). If you'd like to make traditional Buffalo wings, use this sauce in place of the Japanese-Style BBQ Sauce in the Air-Fried Chicken Wings recipe on page 75.

6 tablespoons (¾ stick) unsalted butter, melted

¾ cup medium-hot hot sauce

2 tablespoons honey

Whisk together the butter, hot sauce, and honey in a medium bowl until thoroughly combined. Store in an airtight jar in the refrigerator for up to a month.

PER SERVING:
CALORIES 70 | **PROTEIN** 0g | **CARBS** 2g | **SUGARS** 2g | **FIBER** 0g | **FAT** 7g

TURMERIC TAHINI *Dressing*

YIELD: 1 cup (2 tablespoons per serving) | **PREP TIME:** 8 minutes, plus 4 hours to chill

This anti-inflammatory, golden-colored dressing is a perfect crudité dip. It's also great with the sweet potato fries on page 161.

- ⅓ cup tahini
- ¼ cup lemon juice
- 2 tablespoons extra-virgin olive oil
- 1½ teaspoons maple syrup
- ½ teaspoon cracked black pepper
- ¼ teaspoon Redmond Real Salt
- ¼ teaspoon ground coriander
- ¼ teaspoon ground cumin
- ¼ teaspoon turmeric powder
- Pinch of cayenne pepper
- 2 tablespoons water, plus more if needed

1. Whisk together the tahini, lemon juice, olive oil, maple syrup, black pepper, salt, coriander, cumin, turmeric powder, and cayenne in a medium bowl until smooth and creamy.
2. Whisk in the water, adding more as needed to achieve the desired consistency.
3. Transfer to an airtight container and refrigerate for at least 4 hours before using to allow the flavors to meld. Store in the refrigerator for up to a week.

PER SERVING:
CALORIES 87 | **PROTEIN** 1.6g | **CARBS** 3g | **SUGARS** 1g | **FIBER** 0.6g | **FAT** 8.3g

GREEN TAHINI *Dressing*

YIELD: 1 cup (2 tablespoons per serving) | **PREP TIME:** 5 minutes, plus 4 hours to chill

This dressing is great on salads and animal proteins, or you can mix it into mashed potatoes (see page 155).

⅓ cup tahini

2 tablespoons lemon juice

1 tablespoon extra-virgin olive oil

1 tablespoon apple cider vinegar

¼ cup fresh cilantro leaves

¼ cup fresh Italian parsley leaves

1 tablespoon fresh mint leaves

1 clove garlic, minced

¼ teaspoon Redmond Real Salt

2 tablespoons water, plus more if needed

1. Put the tahini, lemon juice, olive oil, vinegar, cilantro, parsley, mint, garlic, and salt in a blender. Blend on high speed until smooth and creamy.
2. With the blender running on low speed, stream in the water, adding more as needed to achieve the desired consistency.
3. Transfer to an airtight container and refrigerate for at least 4 hours before using to allow the flavors to meld. Store in the refrigerator for up to a week.

PER SERVING:
CALORIES 90 | PROTEIN 2g | CARBS 3g | SUGARS 0g | FIBER 1g | FAT 8g

AVOCADO LIME *Dressing*

YIELD: ¾ cup (2 tablespoons per serving) | **PREP TIME:** 5 minutes, plus 30 minutes to chill

This dressing works well with any taco dish or as a stand-alone for a vegetable dip.

1 ripe avocado, peeled and pitted

3 tablespoons extra-virgin olive oil

Juice of 2 limes

1 clove garlic, peeled

1 tablespoon chopped fresh cilantro leaves

¼ teaspoon ground cumin

¼ teaspoon Redmond Real Salt

2 tablespoons water, plus more if needed

1. Put the avocado, olive oil, lime juice, garlic, cilantro, cumin, and salt in a blender. Blend on high speed until smooth and creamy.
2. With the blender on low speed, stream in the water, adding more as needed to achieve the desired consistency.
3. Transfer the dressing to an airtight container and refrigerate for at least 30 minutes before using. Store in the refrigerator for up to 2 days.

PER SERVING:

CALORIES 90 | PROTEIN 1g | CARBS 3g | SUGARS 0g | FIBER 2g | FAT 8g

BANH MI *Dressing*

YIELD: ⅔ cup (2 tablespoons per serving) | **PREP TIME:** 5 minutes, plus 30 minutes to chill

This Banh Mi Dressing is inspired by the Vietnamese sandwich. This dressing works well on any crunchy salad or as a sauce for seafood.

- 2 tablespoons rice wine vinegar
- 1 tablespoon lime juice
- 1 tablespoon tamari
- 2 teaspoons maple syrup
- 1 clove garlic, minced
- 1 teaspoon grated ginger
- ¼ teaspoon Redmond Real Salt
- ¼ teaspoon red pepper flakes
- 2 tablespoons avocado oil
- 1 tablespoon untoasted sesame oil

1. Whisk together the vinegar, lime juice, tamari, maple syrup, garlic, ginger, salt, and red pepper flakes.
2. Slowly whisk in the oils until the dressing is emulsified.
3. Transfer the dressing to an airtight container and refrigerate for 30 minutes before using. Store in the refrigerator for up to a week.

PER SERVING:
CALORIES 100 | **PROTEIN** 1g | **CARBS** 3g | **SUGARS** 2g | **FIBER** 0g | **FAT** 9g

HIGH-PROTEIN *Caesar Dressing*

YIELD: about 2¾ cups (2 tablespoons per serving) | **PREP TIME:** 8 minutes, plus 4 hours to chill

You won't go back to regular Caesar dressing after you try this recipe because this one is loaded with protein.

- 1 cup plain Greek yogurt (5% fat)
- ½ cup avocado oil mayonnaise
- ½ teaspoon grated lemon zest
- 2 tablespoons lemon juice
- 2 cloves garlic, minced
- 1½ teaspoons anchovy paste
- 1½ teaspoons Dijon mustard
- 1 teaspoon Worcestershire sauce
- 1 cup grated Parmesan cheese
- 2 tablespoons unflavored whey protein powder
- ¼ teaspoon Redmond Real Salt
- ¼ teaspoon cracked black pepper
- ¼ cup water, plus more if needed

1. Put all of the ingredients except the water in a medium bowl and whisk until well combined.
2. Whisk in the water, adding more as needed to achieve the desired consistency.
3. Transfer to an airtight container and refrigerate for at least 4 hours before using to allow the flavors to meld. Store in the refrigerator for up to a week.

PER SERVING:

CALORIES 90 | **PROTEIN** 4g | **CARBS** 1g | **SUGARS** 1g | **FIBER** 0g | **FAT** 7g

HIGH-PROTEIN JALAPEÑO *Ranch Dressing*

YIELD: 1¾ cups (2 tablespoons per serving) | **PREP TIME:** 5 minutes, plus 4 hours to chill

Everyone needs a good recipe for homemade ranch dressing in their repertoire. This one ditches the toxic seed oils found in so many bottled dressings and pumps up the flavor by adding jalapeño. To up the protein even further, you can increase the amount of whey protein powder in this recipe.

- 1 cup plain Greek yogurt (5% fat)
- ¼ cup avocado oil mayonnaise
- ¼ cup full-fat buttermilk
- 1 tablespoon apple cider vinegar
- ¼ cup fresh Italian parsley leaves, chopped
- 2 cloves garlic, minced
- 1 large jalapeño pepper, deveined, seeded, and finely chopped
- 1 teaspoon chopped fresh dill
- 2 tablespoons unflavored whey protein powder
- 1 teaspoon onion powder
- ¼ teaspoon Redmond Real Salt
- 2 tablespoons water, plus more if needed

1. Put all of the ingredients except the water in a medium bowl and whisk until well combined.
2. Whisk in the water, adding more as needed to reach the desired consistency.
3. Transfer the dressing to an airtight container and refrigerate for at least 4 hours, allowing the flavors to meld. Store in the refrigerator for up to a week.

PER SERVING:
CALORIES 60 | **PROTEIN** 3g | **CARBS** 1g | **SUGARS** 1g | **FIBER** 0g | **FAT** 5g

HIGH-PROTEIN *Horseradish Sauce*

YIELD: 1½ cups (2 tablespoons per serving) | **PREP TIME:** 5 minutes, plus 4 hours to chill

This creamy sauce is a great accompaniment for beef or elk tenderloin or even fish. It also makes a terrific salad dressing.

- 1 cup plain Greek yogurt (5% fat)
- ¼ cup avocado oil mayonnaise
- 2 tablespoons unflavored whey protein powder
- 2 tablespoons prepared horseradish
- 1 tablespoon Dijon mustard
- 1 teaspoon apple cider vinegar
- ¼ teaspoon Redmond Real Salt
- ¼ teaspoon cracked black pepper
- 2 tablespoons water, plus more if needed

1. Put all of the ingredients except the water in a medium bowl and whisk until well combined.
2. Whisk in the water, adding more as needed to achieve the desired consistency.
3. Transfer to an airtight container and refrigerate for at least 4 hours before using to allow the flavors to meld. Store in the refrigerator for up to a week.

PER SERVING:
CALORIES 60 | **PROTEIN** 3g | **CARBS** 1g | **SUGARS** 1g | **FIBER** 0g | **FAT** 4g

LEMON DILL
Sauce

YIELD: about 1⅓ cups (2 tablespoons per serving) | **PREP TIME:** 5 minutes, plus 4 hours to chill

This aioli-like sauce is great with fish or poultry.

¾ cup plain Greek yogurt (5% fat)

¼ cup avocado oil mayonnaise

½ teaspoon grated lemon zest

1 tablespoon lemon juice

2 tablespoons finely chopped fresh dill

1 clove garlic, minced

¼ teaspoon onion powder

¼ teaspoon Redmond Real Salt

2 tablespoons water, plus more if needed

1. Put all of the ingredients except the water in a medium bowl and whisk until well combined.
2. Whisk in the water, adding more as needed to achieve the desired consistency.
3. Refrigerate for at least 4 hours before using to allow the flavors to meld. Store in an airtight container in the refrigerator for up to a week.

PER SERVING:
CALORIES 40 | **PROTEIN** 2g | **CARBS** 1g | **SUGARS** 1g | **FIBER** 0g | **FAT** 3g

BACON

YIELD: 1 cup (1 tablespoon per serving) | **PREP TIME:** 6 minutes | **COOK TIME:** 1 hour

This condiment is the perfect accompaniment to beef (see our recipes for Bacon Jam Burger Collard Wraps and Thyme Roasted Marrow Bones with Bacon Jam on pages 97 and 105, respectively). Looking for another use? The next time you make a baked potato, try topping it with bacon jam.

10 ounces thick-cut bacon, cut into ½ inch pieces

1 cup diced yellow onions

⅓ cup maple syrup

¼ cup apple cider vinegar

1. Put the bacon in a large skillet over medium heat and cook, stirring occasionally, until it begins to brown. Stir in the onions and continue cooking until the onions have caramelized and the bacon is crispy, about 25 minutes.
2. Drain off any excess fat. Reduce the heat to low. Pour in the maple syrup and vinegar and cook for 10 minutes, until the mixture thickens.
3. Remove the pan from the heat and allow the jam to cool completely. Store in an airtight container in the refrigerator for up to 2 weeks.

PER SERVING:

CALORIES 60 | **PROTEIN** 1.5g | **CARBS** 4g | **SUGARS** 3g | **FIBER** 0g | **FAT** 4g

SALT RUBS—FIVE WAYS

YIELD: ¼ cup
PREP TIME: 5 minutes

Put all of the ingredients in a small bowl and whisk until combined. Store in an airtight container for up to 6 months (or up to a month for the Chile Lime version due to the fresh lime zest).

Chile Lime Salt Rub

This rub is great on pork or chicken or as a salt rim for a mocktail. For a sweeter rub, double the amount of coconut sugar.

- 2 tablespoons chili powder
- 1 teaspoon coconut sugar
- 1 teaspoon Redmond Real Salt
- ½ teaspoon ground coriander
- ½ teaspoon ground cumin
- ½ teaspoon smoked paprika
- Grated zest of 2 limes

ENTIRE RECIPE:
CALORIES 66 | **PROTEIN** 2.4g | **CARBS** 13.6g | **SUGARS** 6g | **FIBER** 4.8g | **FAT** 2.4g

Everything Bagel Salt Rub

To vary the texture of this rub, try using a coarse salt.

- 1 tablespoon white sesame seeds
- 2 teaspoons black sesame seeds
- 2 teaspoons poppy seeds
- 2 teaspoons dried minced garlic
- 2 teaspoons dried minced onion
- 2 teaspoons Redmond Real Salt

ENTIRE RECIPE:
CALORIES 168 | **PROTEIN** 5.6g | **CARBS** 13g | **SUGARS** 2g | **FIBER** 5.4g | **FAT** 12g

Smoky Steak Salt Rub

If you want more heat in this rub, add a pinch of cayenne pepper.

2 teaspoons chili powder

1½ teaspoons garlic powder

1½ teaspoons onion powder

1½ teaspoons ground cumin

1½ teaspoons dried oregano leaves

1½ teaspoons cracked black pepper

1½ teaspoons cracked white pepper

1¼ teaspoons Redmond Real Salt

½ teaspoon ground coriander

½ teaspoon smoked paprika

ENTIRE RECIPE:
CALORIES 78 | **PROTEIN** 3g | **CARBS** 16.9g | **SUGARS** 3.6g | **FIBER** 5.8g | **FAT** 1.7g

Porchetta Salt Rub

Porchetta is a mouthwatering Italian rolled pork roast. This porchetta-inspired rub is great on pork as well as poultry or fish.

3 tablespoons dried parsley

2 teaspoons ground fennel seed

2 teaspoons Redmond Real Salt

1½ teaspoons dried basil

1½ teaspoons dried celery flakes

1 teaspoon dried oregano leaves

1 teaspoon ground dried rosemary

1 teaspoon ground dried thyme

1 teaspoon garlic powder

1 teaspoon onion powder

½ teaspoon cracked black pepper

ENTIRE RECIPE:
CALORIES 57 | **PROTEIN** 4g | **CARBS** 13.5g | **SUGARS** 1.6g | **FIBER** 5.4g | **FAT** 1.4g

Shawarma Salt Rub

Try this rub on any protein, or season your next potato dish with it.

2 teaspoons ground cumin

2 teaspoons ground fennel seed

2 teaspoons Redmond Real Salt

1½ teaspoons ground coriander

1½ teaspoons turmeric powder

1 teaspoon ground cardamom

1 teaspoon ground cloves

1 teaspoon smoked paprika

½ teaspoon ground cinnamon

ENTIRE RECIPE:
CALORIES 67 | **PROTEIN** 3.4g | **CARBS** 14.8g | **SUGARS** 0.5g | **FIBER** 7.1g | **FAT** 2.9g

RECIPE INDEX

BREAKFASTS

SOUPS AND BROTHS

CHICKEN AND TURKEY

BEEF, BISON, AND LAMB

PORK

VENISON

SEAFOOD

VEGETABLE SIDES

FLATBREADS

DRESSINGS AND SAUCES

GENERAL INDEX

C

D

E

F

G

H

I

J

K

L

M–N

O

P

Q

R

S

T–U

V

W–X

Y–Z

ABOUT THE AUTHORS

Dr. James DiNicolantonio is a Doctor of Pharmacy and a cardiovascular researcher. A well-respected and internationally known scientist and an expert on health and nutrition, he has contributed extensively to health policy. He serves as the associate editor of the *British Medical Journal*'s *Open Heart*, a journal published in partnership with the British Cardiovascular Society, and is on the editorial advisory boards of several other medical journals. He is the author or coauthor of over 300 publications in the medical literature and is the author of nine bestselling health books: *The Salt Fix*, *Superfuel*, *The Longevity Solution*, *The Immunity Fix*, *The Mineral Fix*, *WIN*, *The Obesity Fix*, *The Collagen Cure*, and *The Blood Sugar Fix*. You can follow him on Instagram and Twitter @drjamesdinic and on Facebook at Dr. James DiNicolantonio. His website is drjamesdinic.com.

Tricia Williams is an accomplished chef, nutrition educator, and culinary consultant. In 2018 she founded Daily Dose, a highly customized health supportive meal delivery service for celebrities, elite athletes, and high-performing individuals, so that she could share her passion for fresh, whole, locally grown, organic, sustainable, and delicious food. She believes that what we eat affects our physical, emotional, and mental well-being. Her philosophy is "no gluten, no dairy, no sugar, no problems."

Over the last twenty years, Williams has left her mark on highly regarded Manhattan restaurants including The City Bakery, Home Restaurant, Isla, and Olives. Her passion for culinary nutrition surfaced after she gave birth to her first child. She returned to school to secure her Holistic Nutrition Certification and coupled that with a Food Therapy Certification from holistic health pioneer Annemarie Colbin at the Natural Gourmet Institute. She does a lot of consulting work, including product and menu development for health food brands. One of her favorite projects to date was working on Hu Kitchen's menu before it opened.

Williams's recipes can be found in Dr. David Perlmutter's book *Drop Acid*, in Dr. Frank Lipman's book *10 Reasons You Get Old and Feel Fat*, at Bon Appetit online, and in her "Junk Food Makeover" column on Yahoo Health. Her wisdom on healthy fat appears in Bobbi Brown's book *Beauty from the Inside Out*, and she is a recurring judge on the TV show *Beat Bobby Flay*.